East African Wildlife Guide

A *fun* introduction to the animals of
Kenya, Tanzania,
Rwanda, Uganda and Burundi

Birgit Hendry

Copyright © 2024 Birgit Hendry

All rights reserved. No portion of this book may be reproduced, copied, distributed or adapted in any way, with the exception of certain activities permitted by applicable copyright laws, such as brief quotations in the context of a review or academic work. For permission to publish, distribute or otherwise reproduce this work, please contact the author at birgit@wildsights.com

Published independently in the United Kingdom by Wildsights Publishing
www.wildsights.com
First Edition, 2024

Text & Design:	Birgit Hendry
Editors:	Wayne Hendry, Suzie Andrade
Maps:	Mike Shand & Birgit Hendry, created using data with permission from the International Union for Conservation of Nature (IUCN); www.iucn.org (see detailed credits page 188)
Drawings:	Wayne & Birgit Hendry
Photos:	See detailed photo credits page 184

Title of the Book: East African Wildlife Guide - A fun introduction to the animals of Kenya, Tanzania, Rwanda, Uganda and Burundi

ISBN 978-1-0686434-1-5

Although this publication is designed to provide accurate information in regard to the subject matter covered, the publisher and the author assume no responsibility for errors, inaccuracies, omissions, or any other inconsistencies herein. This publication is meant as a source of valuable information for the reader, however it is not meant as a replacement for direct expert assistance. If such level of assistance is required, the services of a competent professional should be sought.

for Sean & Ciara

who inspired me to write this book

Contents

Acknowledgements... 8

Foreword... 10

Introduction... 12

A few lessons from Africa... 13

East Africa... 14

The big icons... 16
Buffalo... 18
African Elephant... 20
Giraffe... 22
Rhinoceros... 24

Spiral-horned antelopes... 26
Eland... 28
Greater Kudu... 30
Lesser Kudu... 32
Sitatunga... 34
Bushbuck... 36
Eastern Bongo... 38

Larger antelopes & zebra... 40
Waterbuck... 42
Sable Antelope... 44
Roan Antelope... 46
Wildebeest... 48
Zebra... 50

Medium antelopes... 52
Impala... 54
Topi... 56
Puku... 58
Hartebeest... 60
Reedbuck... 62
Ugandan Kob... 64

Smaller antelopes... 66
Dik-dik... 68
Duiker... 70
Steenbok... 72
Klipspringer... 74
Oribi... 76
Suni... 78
Sharpe's Grysbok... 79

Cats & cat-likes... 80
Lion... 82
Leopard... 84
Cheetah... 86
Serval... 88
Caracal... 89
African Wildcat... 90
African Golden Cat... 91
Genet... 92
Civet... 93

Other predators... 94
Hyena... 96
African Wild Dog... 98
Bat-eared Fox... 100
Jackal... 102
African Golden Wolf... 104
Honey Badger... 105

Maasailand... 106
Gerenuk... 108
Thomson's Gazelle... 110
East African Oryx... 112
Grant's Gazelle... 114

In the Water... 116
Hippopotamus... 118
Nile Crocodile... 120
Otter... 122

Apes & Monkeys... 124
Vervet monkey... 126
Baboon... 128
A few more monkeys... 130
Chimpanzee... 132
Gorilla... 134

Night visitors... 136
Aardvark... 138
Pangolin... 139
Hedgehog... 140
Porcupine... 141
Zorilla & African Striped Weasel... 142
Bushbaby & Galago... 143

Pigs... 144
Bushpig... 146
Warthog... 147
Giant Forest Hog... 148
Red River Hog... 149

The little guys... 150
Hyrax... 152
Mongoose... 153
Mole, Shrew, Gerbil, Mouse & Rat... 154
Squirrel... 156
Hare & Rabbit... 157

Some scaly creatures... 158
Lizard & Chameleon... 160
Tortoise, Terrapin & Turtle... 162
Snake... 164

Wings and feathers... 166
Bat... 168
Ostrich... 170
Birds - a selection... 172

Some "show-off" words... 176

Credits... 184

Bibliography... 193

Acknowledgements

It took me many years to complete this project and I could not have done it without the help of my family and a few people I crossed paths with along the way.

Special thanks to...

My late parents, who sparked my interest in nature and Africa.

Mike Shand, Cartographer and Honorary Research Fellow, School of Geographical & Earth Sciences, University of Glasgow. We met in Arusha, Tanzania, in 2004 on a map design course he was running. Mike was instrumental in the map design for this book.

Craig Hilton-Taylor, Head Red List Unit, Biodiversity Assessment & Knowledge Team, Science & Data Centre, International Union for Conservation of Nature (IUCN), who allowed me to use the IUCN Red List data to create my maps.

Suzie Andrade, my Kenyan friend, who proof-read this book and, with her knowledge of Africa and the English language, gave me some very valuable input.

Petra Meyr, safari expert and my neighbour in Arusha, who introduced me to African People & Wildlife, the charity this book supports.

Katy Teson, Communications and Outreach Manager at African People & Wildlife, who wrote the foreword.

The following children:

Annina Leavey (age 13), Hamish Ostroumoff-Croucher (12), Aubrey Poett (10), Hamish Wollensack-Kotlewski (10), Rafe Leavey (9), Lewis Wollensack-Kotlewski (8), Aubrey Ostroumoff-Croucher (8), Margo Poett (7), Rhys Wollensack-Kotlewski (7) and Mary Poett (6) for their input. They checked the maps with enthusiasm and helped me to ensure that they were understandable for young minds.

My husband Wayne, walking encyclopaedia on African wildlife, photographer, and artist, for his drawings, photos, knowledge, and inspiration.

Last but not least, all the staff in the various safari camps I visited over the years, who indirectly encouraged and supported my passion for the African bush... asanteni sana!

Foreword

Welcome to the world of African wildlife! As you journey through the pages of this book, you're also supporting something special: the environmental education programmes of African People & Wildlife. Founded in 2005 by Dr. Laly Lichtenfeld and Charles Trout, African People & Wildlife is dedicated to protecting wildlife, investing in people, and restoring balance to Africa's vital ecosystems - now powered by a team of 200+ Tanzanian scientists, educators, programme officers, and community members! At the heart of their vision lies the belief that Africa's people and wildlife can thrive together in vibrant, healthy landscapes.

Imagine a place where communities and wildlife are deeply connected, where every action benefits both people and the planet. That's the world African People & Wildlife is striving to create in Tanzania, and the purchase of this book supports the work to make it a reality.

Through education programmes, young minds are introduced to the intricacies of local wildlife ecology through after-school wildlife clubs. Students experience the excitement of once-in-a-lifetime field trips to Tarangire National Park, witnessing the beauty of lions and other wild animals in their natural habitat. Week-long summer camps at the Noloholo Environmental Center offer a chance to be immersed in the landscape and explore the outdoors with wildlife experts. These programmes are creating conservation leaders today, right now, to help build a better, greener future.

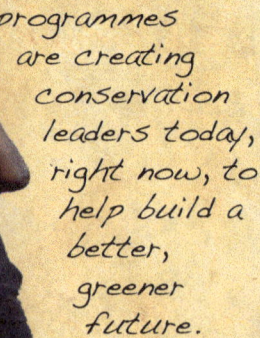

Education is the bridge that connects us to the wonders of nature and our role as conservationists. It opens our eyes to the interconnectedness of all living things and empowers us to become stewards of the environment. As you read these pages, you're also becoming part of a movement to ensure that future generations can continue to marvel at the diversity of East Africa's wildlife and wild places.

So, join the adventure, embrace the joy of discovery, and let the pages of this book be your guide into the places and creatures we all cherish.

Katy Teson

African People & Wildlife

Introduction

As a child growing up in Germany, my favourite TV shows were 'A Place for Wild Animals' by Prof. Dr. Bernhard Grzimek, famous for his documentary 'Serengeti shall not die' and 'Expeditions into the Animal Kingdom' by Heinz Sielmann. My dream was to live in the African bush, and after spending a year in South Africa and completing my studies of geography, I bought a one-way ticket to Kilimanjaro airport. Arriving in Tanzania felt like a home-coming, and I ended up living there for the next 13 years, working in conservation while raising a family.

Our children were privileged to have iconic places such as the Serengeti and the Ngorongoro Crater on their door step, and they grew up camping in Maasailand, on safari in Tarangire National Park or barefoot in our garden. They are the ones who inspired me to write this book.

Most wilderness areas in Africa have no mobile phone connection and definitely no "Gs", as my son would call it – neither 5G nor 4G or even 3G – not even mobile phone reception... and that is great. 😊 You are forced to immerse yourself into the sights, sounds and smells of the bush and use a good old-fashioned book for information – even if it is an e-book. However, many great safari guides are often very detailed and written for adults, while most wildlife books for children only talk about well-known animals such as elephants, giraffes and lions. This book is something inbetween – while it covers all mammals (I hope I didn't forget any) that can be found in East Africa, plus a few large reptiles and birds, it is meant to be fun and does not require a degree in zoology to understand 😊 – after all, we can only protect what we understand.

"No one will protect what they don't care about; and no one will care about what they have never experienced."
Sir David Attenborough

My wish is that children, teenagers and adults of all ages will enjoy this book – whether reading it at home dreaming of Africa, or, for the lucky ones, using it as their guide book on a safari.

A few lessons from Africa

- The smallest termite is as fascinating as the majestic elephant, and the 'ugly' hyena is as important as the 'beautiful' cheetah – all creatures have their place in the circle of life (and hyenas are NOT ugly 😊).

- Animals in the wild can be dangerous, respect their space.

- Even though it may look cruel when a lion kills an antelope, remember – lions need to eat too.

- To protect wildlife, the most important thing is to look after the places they live in – their habitat.

- When you are in nature, leave ONLY your footprints behind – anywhere in the world, not only in Africa.

- Respect the people who live alongside wild and dangerous animals.

- Don't feed wild animals on safari. Food that is good for people is not good for animals. Wild animals are not pets – they could become aggressive.

East Africa

- In this book, East Africa includes five countries: Tanzania, Kenya, Uganda, Rwanda and Burundi.

- The peaks of the four highest mountains in Africa are located in East Africa:
  1. Mount Kilimanjaro (Tanzania)
  2. Mount Kenya (Kenya)
  3. Mount Stanley (Uganda)
  4. Mount Meru (Tanzania)

- East Africa is home to some famous conservation areas, such as:
  Tanzania: Serengeti National Park, Ngorongoro Crater Conservation Area, Tarangire, Manyara and Ruaha National Parks, Nyerere National Park (part of the original Selous Game Reserve).
  Kenya: Tsavo and Amboseli National Parks, Samburu and Maasai Mara National Reserves.
  Uganda: Murchison Falls, Queen Elizabeth and Bwindi Impenetrable Forest National Parks.
  Rwanda: Volcanoes, Akagera and Nyungwe National Parks, Mukura Forest Reserve.
  Burundi: Kibira, Rusizi and Ruvubu National Parks.

- Dozens of different languages and dialects are spoken in East Africa, but many people speak Swahili as their first or second language. The headings for each animal in this book are in English with their Swahili names mentioned below.

Kilimanjaro Uhuru peak: 5895m

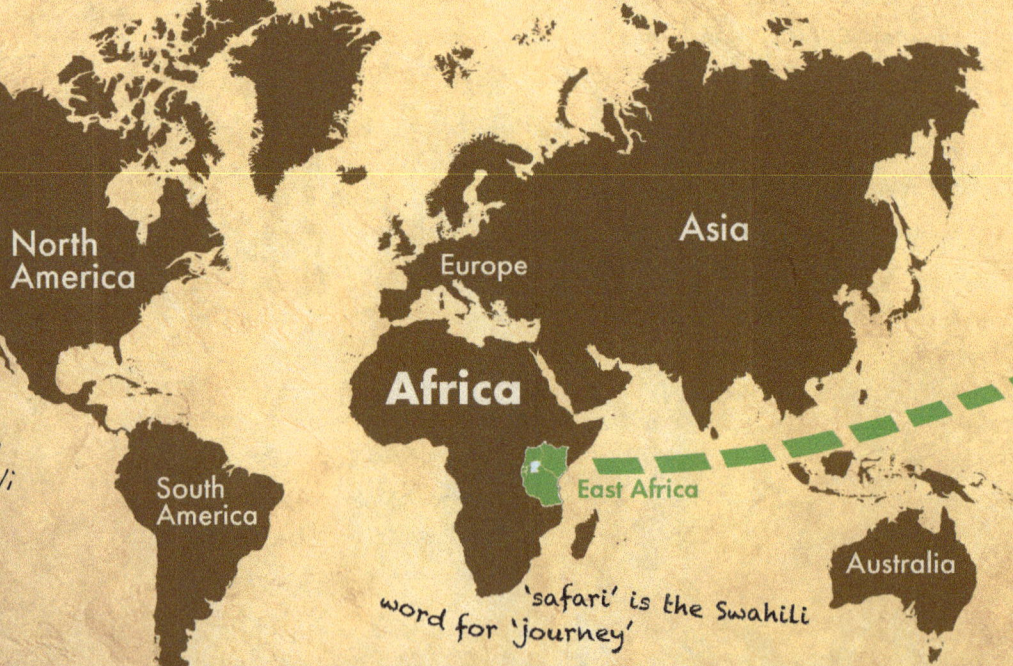

'safari' is the Swahili word for 'journey'

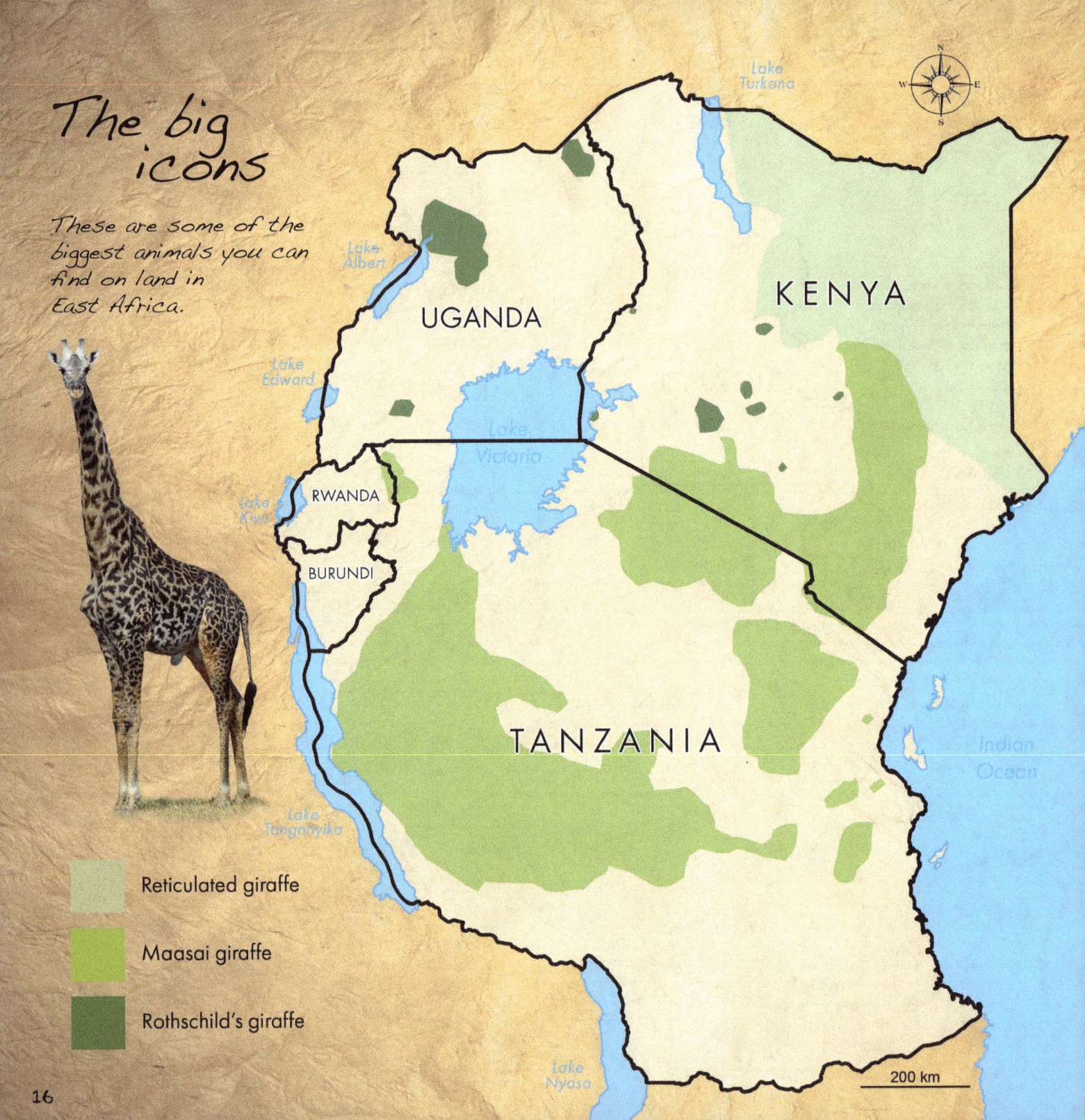

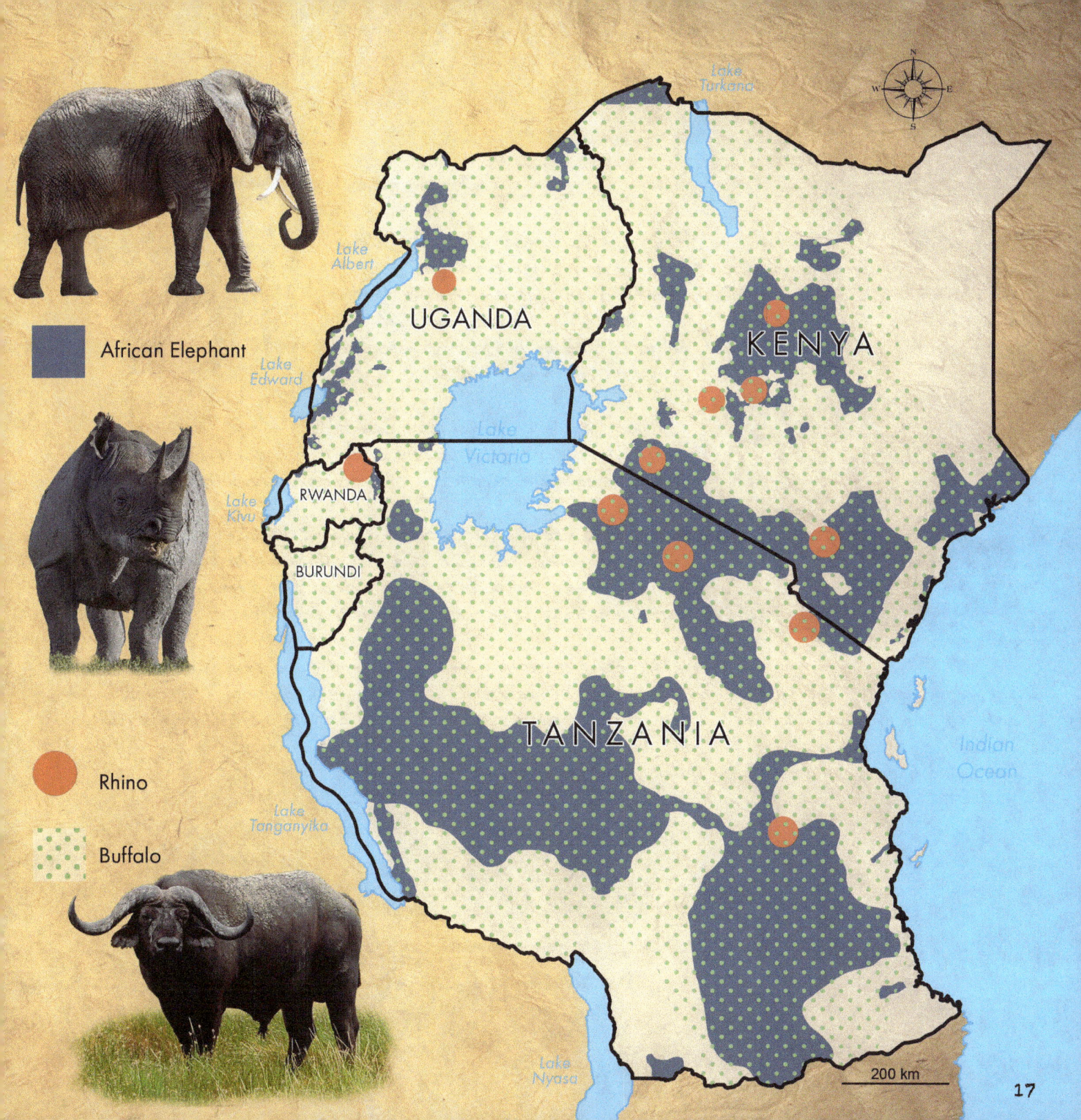

Buffalo
mbogo / nyati

If you spot an animal in the African wilderness that is bulky, black or dark brown and looks like a cow, then this will most definitely be a Cape or African buffalo (in Uganda they call it a Nile buffalo). They are just about as tall as a person, but more than ten times as heavy. Both females and males carry massive horns on their heads.

These huge animals love tall grass - not just to eat but also to hide in - and they like a good mud bath too; the mud protects them from annoying insects.

Buffalo are always found close to water as they need to drink every day. In the dry season they might have to walk a long way to find food, but they will always return to a water hole or river to quench their thirst.

Buffalo usually live in big herds and they are very social animals. If there is enough food, some herds are over 1500 animals strong. When they lie down to rest, they usually separate into little groups. Old male buffalo (you can recognize them by their heavy, solid, deeply curved horns) leave the herd and live together in so-called bachelor herds.

You might find a buffalo skull like this one in the bush – imagine how heavy it would be to carry those horns on your head all day...

Buffalo can run faster than lions, but they are a bit slow to start with, so they have to really watch out for lions sneaking up on them. When buffalo stay with their herds, it is difficult for lions to hunt them. Sometimes buffalo even fight back, and lions have to run away so they don't get trampled or hooked by the huge horns.

bull after a mud bath

Oxpeckers are the buffalo's private cleaners, they spend the day picking insects off the buffalo's body. They benefit from each other – this is called 'symbiosis'

🐾 Interesting fact: Although buffalo often come across as being sleepy and very tame, they can be very dangerous when you try to approach them – they are not as nice as their cow cousins, and they can easily outrun you!

buffalo tracks

African Elephant
tembo / ndovu

The elephant is the largest land animal in the world. Bulls (males) weigh up to 7,000 kilograms, which is as heavy as four family cars. At birth a baby elephant already weighs more than an adult man.

There are two species of elephant in Africa, and the one that you can find in East Africa is called the bush or savanna elephant. The savanna elephant is the biggest of all elephants in the world - adults are over three meters tall.

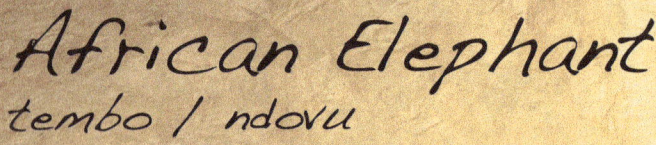
elephant dung - it can be used to make paper

The coolest thing about elephants are their trunks. They can pick up tiny fruit with them or break off high branches to get to the juicy leaves at the top. They also use the trunks for many other things like drinking, greeting or threatening each other, fighting and most importantly, smelling. An elephant can suck up to 14 litres of water into its trunk at a time, which it then squirts into its mouth to drink.

'mock charge'

this elephant is pretending to attack, it opens its ears to look bigger

Another important tool for elephants is their tusks. They use them to dig for water and roots, to pull bark off trees, and bulls use them to fight each other. Tusks can grow to over three meters long and weigh over 90 kilograms (the weight of a baby elephant 😊)... imagine having to carry those around with you all day... elephants are certainly very strong animals.

When an elephant cow is pregnant — yes, an elephant female is called 'cow' — she carries the baby for 22 months before it is born. After birth, the mother and other cows in the herd all look after the baby elephant — there is a very strong bond between elephants and their mothers, which lasts many years. Mothers often hold their babies' tails to guide them, or the babies hold their mothers' tails when they follow them. Elephants are very social animals.

🐾 Interesting fact:
Elephants sleep very little, possibly only two to four hours a day. Researchers think that this is because they are so big and need to eat most of the time to keep up their weight. They can eat well over 100 kilograms of fruit, grasses, bark and roots a day.

elephant tracks

Giraffe
twiga

The giraffe is the tallest land animal in the world. It can grow more than five meters tall, which is about three times as tall as an adult person. Giraffes have very long necks, which they need to reach their food high up in the trees. Their tongues are about half a meter long, which helps them to pick out the greenest leaves between thorns, especially in their favourite acacia trees - imagine, their tongues are longer than your arm...

Giraffes spend a lot of time feeding. They need plenty of food because they are so large - over 30 kilograms of leaves every day. With every bite, they only manage to grab a few leaves, so no fast food for giraffes. ☺

Giraffes have very good eyes

Most herd animals have leaders and stay close together for security, but giraffe herds don't. Giraffes are so big that not many predators dare to attack them, especially not the adults.

giraffe tracks

Mother giraffes go back to the same place to give birth and they look after their calves for over a year. The mothers watch their babies very carefully and even defend them against lions, kicking the lions with their hooves. If they have to leave them for a while, the baby giraffes stay in a "giraffe nursery" where other herd members watch them. This is called "a crèche".

a thorny lunch

reticulated giraffe

a special way to drink...

There are many different kinds of giraffe, called "subspecies". They vary in size, colour, have all kinds of patterns and they occur in different parts of Africa. In East Africa you can see the Maasai, the reticulated, the Nubian and the Rothschild's giraffe.

It is great to see a giraffe run; it looks like a movie in slow motion. Another cool thing is the way they drink. You would not believe it but their necks are too short, they need to just about go into a split with their front legs to reach the water... not easy. Good thing they don't need to drink too often as they get most of the moisture they need from their food.

🐾 **Interesting fact:** Despite their long necks, which can be over two meters long, giraffes have exactly as many neck bones, called vertebrae, as people... only seven.

Maasai giraffe, Tanzania

giraffe crèche

Rhinoceros
kifaru

The full name of this herbivore is actually rhinoceros, but it is easier to just call it rhino.

There are two different species of rhinos in East Africa – black rhinos and white rhinos; they are quite different from each other in many ways. White rhinos are about twice as heavy as black rhinos. White rhinos have a very broad mouth, which helps them to eat grass, they are grazers – that's why they are also called "square-lipped rhinos". The black rhino's mouth is pointy, it looks a bit like a beak – so sometimes it is called "hook-lipped rhino". Black rhinos are browsers, so they use the pointy mouth to pull leaves off bushes. White rhinos are usually more social and live in groups while black rhinos prefer to be by themselves.

Unfortunately there are very few rhinos left in East Africa – and if you get to see one you are very lucky as they only occur in a few places and in very low numbers, often living in the protection of sanctuaries.

There are a few theories, but nobody is sure why they are called black and white rhinos, it has nothing to do with their colour, they are both grey - unless they are covered in mud. ☺

Rhinos have two horns on their noses; the one that is closer to the mouth is much bigger than the second one behind. They use them for digging, breaking off bark from trees and for fighting other rhinos.

There is a funny thing rhinos do when they want to tell other rhinos that they are around - they poo on the paths they walk on or on the boundaries of the territories they live in. When a rhino finds a poo pile from another rhino, it digs in it with its horns, kicks it with its hind feet and scatters it around.

🐾 Interesting fact: Rhinos can't see very well - so if you happen to see a rhino in the bush when you are on foot, it is safer not to move!

white rhino calf with mother

rhino tracks

black rhino - check the beak-shaped mouth

Eland
pofu

The eland is the largest antelope in the world. Male elands can weigh over 600 kilograms - the same weight as a big horse. They have straight spiralled horns, which the males use to fight off rivals, and females use to chase away predators from their young.

The colour of the eland's coat is tan or grey. Males get darker as they get older and a thick mop of hair grows on their foreheads. They also have a big flap of skin hanging down from their necks - this is called a dewlap.

You can find elands in herds of up to 500 animals.

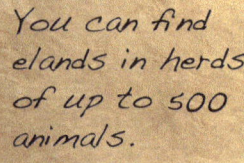

They live in open plains and woodlands, where there are plenty of grasses, leaves and flowers to feed on.

Elands are not territorial, they are nomadic, which means they move from one place to another to find food.

dewlap

Apart from being the biggest, elands are also the slowest antelope in the world, and they can't run fast for long distances – but they can jump easily over a three-meter-high fence.

🐾 **Interesting fact:** You often hear a loud clicking sound when you are close to a herd of elands. Researchers are not sure yet where this comes from, but they believe that the sound is made when the two parts of the hooves snap together as the heavy eland lifts a foot.

female

male

front   back

eland tracks

29

Greater Kudu
tandala kubwa

If you would like to see a greater kudu, look out for them in between the trees and bushes. Despite being the second tallest antelope in Africa, it is surprisingly difficult to spot one. Kudus live in small herds and like to hide in the brush. They have white stripes on their sides which help them to be camouflaged - when they stand still, they blend very well into their surroundings.

Kudus are browsers, but they also like to eat tubers, flowers and herbs. If they are not able to find water, they get moisture from eating fruit.

When kudus run away from danger, they can jump very high. They could easily jump over a car, and sometimes even higher. Their big spiral horns point back when they run and their tails fan out white as a warning signal to predators who might be following them.

male adult

kudu horns at   1 year   18 months   2 years   3 years   over 4 years   over 8 years old

kudu tracks

young kudu male

female adult

Both male and female kudus have giant ears, but only male kudus have those beautiful spiral horns. When the horns start to grow, they are short and straight. The older the kudu gets, the longer the horns are and the more curves they have. The longest kudu horns ever measured were over 180 centimetres long, measured along the curl of the horns. They were found in Mozambique.

Kudus make one of the loudest barks in the antelope world. They can also hear, see and smell really well.

🐾 Interesting fact: The Maasai in East Africa use kudu horns to communicate between villages. They drill a hole into the thinner part of the horn and blow into it to make a loud hooting noise.

Lesser Kudu
tandala ndogo

This elegant antelope is only found in East Africa and Ethiopia. It looks like a small version of the greater kudu. Females and young lesser kudus have a reddish coat. The males' coat turns grey after they are two years old and both, males and females, have bold white stripes down the sides of their bodies, which are more obvious than on a greater kudu. Only males have spectacular spiral horns, but they rarely use them for fighting and if they do, the fight is most of the times not serious. Adult males usually live by themselves while females stay in small groups with their calves.

Lesser kudus are browsers and live primarily in thickly wooded, dry and shady areas with short grass, where they blend well into their surroundings. It can be very difficult to spot them - look out for a moving ear or tail. They feed at dusk or dawn and do not need any water to drink as they get all the liquid they need through the plants they eat.

Like the males of many other animal species, lesser kudu males can smell when a female is ready for breeding. The female pees when a male touches her and the male "tests" the pee to see if the female is ready to fall pregnant - seriously. Males and females only stay together during mating season, after that they go their own ways. The female is pregnant for about eight months.

lesser kudu female

At the end of her pregnancy the lesser kudu cow leaves her group and gives birth to a calf, which weighs only about as much as a pet cat. The calf stays hidden in the bush while the mother leaves to feed. She comes back a few times a day. She then first smells the calf – this is to make sure that it is her baby – then she cleans it and lets it suckle. After a couple of weeks, the calf joins the group with its mother.

lesser kudu tracks

Lesser kudus are very shy. When they sense danger, they stand completely still to listen with their big ears. If they hear a predator approach, they make warning barking noises and flee through the thicket in leaps, jumping up to two meters high.

🐾 Interesting fact: The lesser kudu is said to be the most beautiful antelope in Africa – do you agree?

Sitatunga
nzohe

The sitatunga is an antelope that lives in swamps and marshes. It prefers areas with thick vegetation to hide in and walk on - sitatungas are very well adjusted to that kind of habitat. They have long, thin hooves, which allow them to walk through the mud and water without sinking. On dry land they can be quite clumsy.

These antelopes are very good swimmers. When they feel threatened, they run into the water and even hide under the surface with only their noses sticking out for air.

female

Sitatungas have a waterproof, oily, shaggy coat which is perfectly suited to wet areas. Only the males have corkscrew like horns and a shaggy mane.

young bull

sitatunga bull

These rare antelopes feed on many different plants that are found in their watery homes.

Sitatungas often use the same paths and tunnels through the vegetation in the swamps where they live. When they want to rest, they get onto small floating islands or dry hills in the reeds. They keep walking in circles until they have trampled the grass down and made it into a nice soft mattress. This is also where the females give birth to their calves.

Unlike most other antelopes, sitatungas are solitary — this means they don't live in big herds, but mostly on their own. Even their young become independent quite early on; they can look after themselves already at six months of age.

🐾 Interesting fact: The sitatunga's back legs are longer than its front legs — that's why they look somewhat hunched over.

sitatunga calf

sitatunga tracks

front   back

Bushbuck
pongo

The beautiful bushbuck is widespread in many countries in Africa, but can still be pretty hard to find. It lives in and around forests and blends in very well with the bushes and trees.
Bushbuck are browsers, but they also eat fruit, bark, flowers, herbs and other plants, in fact they spend most of their time feeding. You can usually spot them in the early morning, but in some areas, especially close to people, they are completely nocturnal. Bushbuck are mostly solitary animals, which means they prefer to stay alone.

It is very important to a bushbuck mother to hide her calf in the bush after birth. She prepares and cleans a safe place and leaves it alone there for many hours every day. She returns a few times per day to feed and play with it - they love to run around and chase each other. Only once the calf is four months old does it follow the mother more often and for longer periods of time. Until then the calf spends most of its time motionless and quiet in its hiding place... a small human child would not be able to do that for very long.

bushbuck male

bushbuck calf

A Bushbuck is not territorial – it is the only antelope in Africa which does not defend a territory. Even so, males tend to challenge other males to a fight, especially if there is a female on heat in the area. They start to walk in a stiff kind of way, lift their heads and tails, arch their backs and circle each other. If one of the two males gives up he licks the adversary. If they end up fighting, they try to stab each other with their horns. Sometimes even females fight each other.

🐾 Interesting fact: To protect their young, bushbuck mothers eat their dung so that predators can't smell it.

bushbuck female
they have no horns

bushbuck tracks

Eastern Bongo
bongo

Even though bongos are very big antelopes with a bright red coat and white stripes, it is difficult to spot them. They can be well camouflaged in the jungle. The older they get, the darker their coats become, and the males' coat is darker than the females'.

Bongos are nocturnal and live in very dense rain forest. There are two species of bongo in Africa, the western or lowland bongo in western and central Africa and the eastern or mountain bongo in East Africa. There are only a few small areas in Kenya where you can find the mountain bongo and there are very few of them left in the wild.

Both male and female bongos have horns, which can grow up to a meter long. When bongos run away, they flatten their horns against their backs, so it is easier for them to dodge the plants in the dense forest. Sometimes they get bald patches from the horns rubbing against their backs.

Adult males normally live by themselves while females and young bongos stay together in small groups. Bulls meet with females only for mating. When the females are ready to give birth, they often go back to the same area where they have given birth before. Like many antelopes, the bongo mother hides her calf for the first few weeks of its life. She visits a few times a day to suckle her new-born. After a short time, bongo calves join their mothers and other young bongos.

bongo calf

When a bongo is scared, it runs away surprisingly fast, considering that it has to find a way through the thick jungle growth. Then they hide, with their back facing the danger - this way they can easily continue to run if they need to.

Bongos are browsers, using their long tongues to feed on leaves, bark, fruit, herbs, and roots, and need to drink regularly. Sometimes they eat burnt wood after a fire or visit natural salt licks to cover their need for minerals and salt.

bongo tracks

🐾 Interesting fact: Apparently the red-brown colour of the bongo rubs off quite easily. People say that rainwater running over the bongo's coat is tinted red... if you happen to see a bongo in the rain, you can check if that's true. ☺

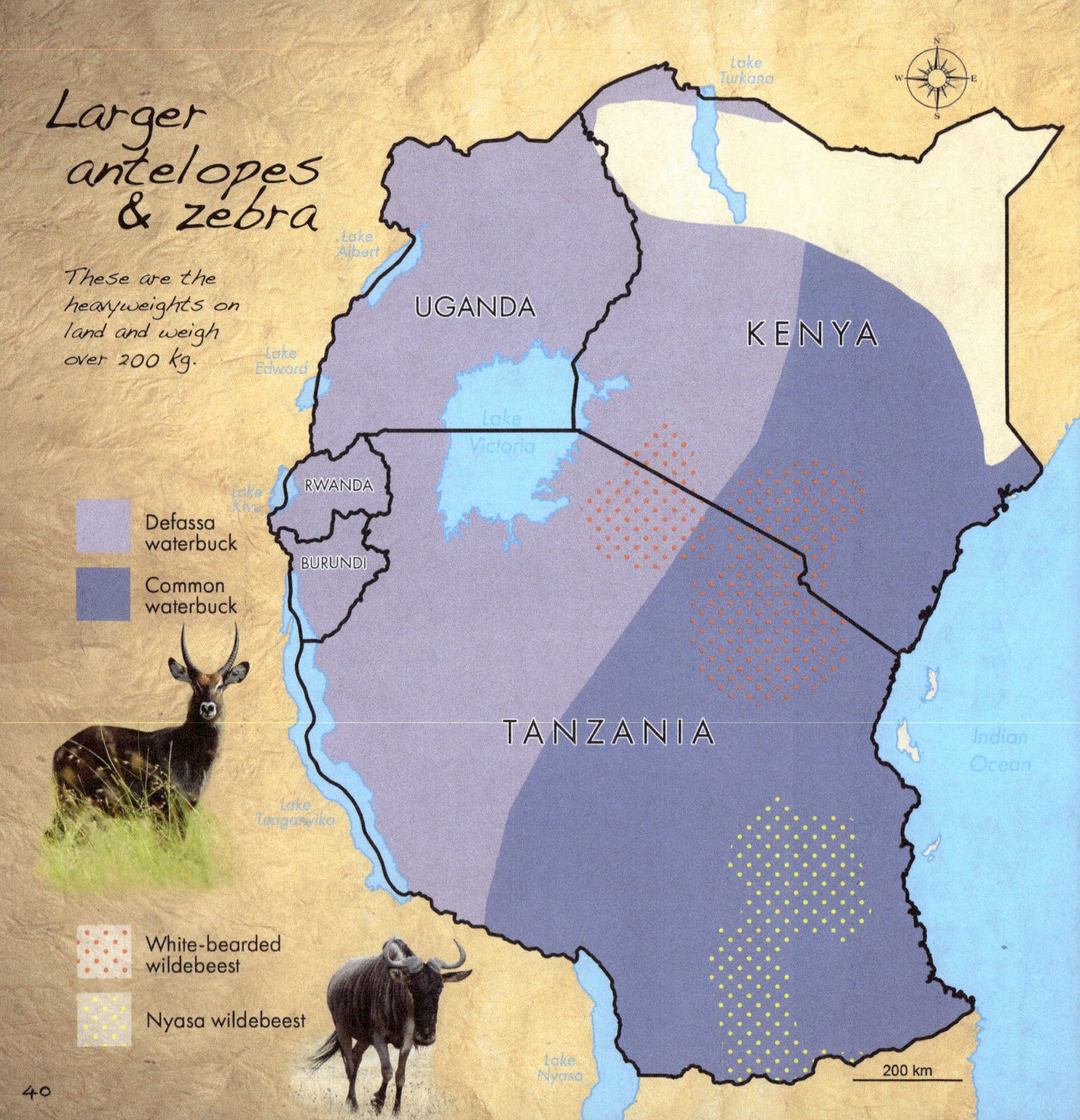

Waterbuck
kuro

With its shaggy, coarse coat a waterbuck appears more geared for the snow than for the hot savanna sun - this animal looks so different from other African antelopes. In East Africa there are two subspecies, the common waterbuck and the Defassa waterbuck. The common ones have a white circle around their bums - that's why they are also called "ringed waterbuck" - the others don't. With age the fur of a waterbuck gets darker. Only male waterbuck have horns.

This antelope is called a waterbuck as it likes living close to water - obvious, right? 😊 It has to drink every one or two days, mainly feeds on grass and sometimes herbs and leaves, usually in the morning and in the evening. Waterbuck often eat tough grasses that other antelopes don't like.

Waterbuck don't live in the water, but they sometimes run into the water to escape from predators.

They are sedentary antelopes, which means they don't migrate.

Defassa youngster

Defassa waterbuck male

Defassa female

Waterbuck are not very fast and they can't run for very long either, so rather than running away they try and hide if there is danger. Even waterbuck babies stay hidden in the bush for a quite while after birth, but their mothers are never far away from them. When they are a bit bigger, they join a group of youngsters, called a crèche.

🐾 Interesting fact: Waterbuck have sweat glands that make their fur stinky. This is supposed to keep predators away.

waterbuck tracks

common waterbuck male

common waterbuck female and calf

Sable Antelope
palahala

Sable antelopes are mainly grazers, but they also eat leaves, especially in the dry season. They are very selective when they eat and prefer certain grasses. Sometimes they pick up and chew old bones, which provide their bodies with certain minerals. You can find sables in savanna woodlands and grasslands and they are never very far from water.

Sables are beautiful antelopes, they come in all shades of brown, and old bulls are a shiny black colour. The fur of new-born calves matches the colour of dry grass, which makes them harder for predators to spot.

Like many antelopes, sable females can have calves once they are only two years old. When the calf is born, the mother hides with it in the bush until it is old enough to follow the herd.

sable bulls fighting

sable tracks

sable about a year old

Twice a day the calf gets suckled by its mother. After the feeding, the calf will move to a new place to hide. It does that to make it harder for predators to find the little one as they can smell the poo and pee it leaves behind. After about four weeks, the calf walks, plays and sleeps with the herd.

Both male and female sables have long curved horns. A bull's horns can easily be longer than 100 centimetres.

Sable bulls often fight each other for dominance, which means the winner will be the boss of the herd. When the bulls fight, they drop to their knees and use their long, curved horns to attack each other. They rarely get hurt during a fight.

🐾 **Interesting fact:** Sable antelopes even confront predators such as lions and fight them off using their horns.

Roan Antelope
korongo

Roan antelopes are named after the colour "roan", which is a reddish brown. With their black and white mask-like markings on their faces, they resemble sable antelopes a little bit. Both males and females carry horns, and they have enormous ears.

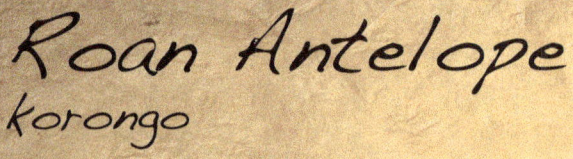

Roan are mainly grazers, but they also feed on some herbs and leaves.

Like all other antelopes, roan are ruminants. This means they eat and swallow grass or leaves and in the first part of their stomachs, they digest the food with the help of bacteria. Then they regurgitate the food, which means the food gets transported back up into their mouths. The "food" is then called "the cud". They settle down and chew it again and again to make it even smaller and softer - this is called "ruminating". You might have seen cows on farms doing the same thing.

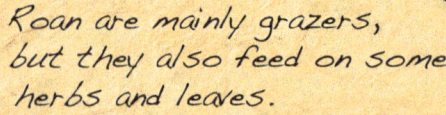

Roan antelopes are territorial, the males defend their territories against other male antelopes.

When female roan calves grow up, they generally stay in the same area, but young male roan get thrown out of the herd by the dominant male when they are a few years old. They then stay together in so-called bachelor herds until they are about six years of age and are able to start their own herds. Most antelope species behave in a similar way.

roan tracks

Roan antelopes can be quite aggressive. They defend their herds even against predators as big as lions, using their curved horns as weapons to threaten and chase them away.

If you want to find roan antelopes, look out for them in the open savanna and tall grass or areas that are covered with a few trees.

🐾 Interesting fact: Roan antelopes are anti-social and don't like to be around other antelopes.

Wildebeest
nyumbu

Nyasa wildebeest

white-bearded wildebeest

There are two different subspecies of wildebeest in East Africa - the Nyasa wildebeest with a white stripe across its face in southern Tanzania and the white-bearded wildebeest in northern Tanzania and Kenya.

Some people say that wildebeest are ugly. They sort of look as if they were put together from body parts of other animals - but they have a lot of character. At first, they look grey, but in the sun their furs look glossy and reveal a metallic sheen.

Wildebeest are also called "gnu" as the noise they are making sounds a bit like "gnoooo". If you are lucky enough to witness the Great Migration in Kenya and Tanzania, where thousands of wildebeest travel on their search for food and water every year, listen to all of them "gnooooing"... it is an amazing experience.

Nyasa wildebeest

horn shape of a young gnu... ...and an adult one

Gnus eat lots of grass and need to be close to water so they can drink every day or two. They are ruminants, which means they chew and swallow the grass they eat, then regurgitate it and chew it again. Sounds yummy. ⓦ

One thing that is special about wildebeest is that all their calves are born together, within a few weeks after the rains have arrived, when there is lots of fresh grass. A few minutes after birth the little ones can run, and they always stay close to their mothers – that is a good thing as wildebeest live in open grasslands with no place to hide from predators.

🐾 Interesting fact: When it is the time of year for wildebeest to mate, the bulls jump, buck and rub their heads on the ground and do all kinds of funny things to mark their territories. That is why they are often called "clowns of the savanna".

gnu tracks

Zebra
punda milia

Zebras look somewhat like horses in pyjamas. In Swahili, the language many people speak in East Africa, a zebra is called a "punda milia", which means "striped donkey". The black and white stripes on a zebra are different from any other zebra and as unique as a human fingerprint.

Grevy zebra

There are two different species of zebra in East Africa - the plains and the Grevy's zebra. They differ from each other in their stripe patterns and size. The most common one in East Africa is the plains zebra. The adults' stripes are crisp black and white, and the young ones have fluffy brown stripes - they often look a bit dirty.

People have many ideas as to why zebras have stripes. Some say the stripes confuse predators, keep biting flies off or help to control the zebra's temperature; others say zebras can recognise each other by their stripes as the stripe patterns are all unique. Maybe it's a bit of everything - any ideas?

plains zebra

Zebras are very social animals and usually live in herds of females and youngsters protected by a male zebra, called a stallion.

They travel a lot in search of food and water and are part of the famous Great Migration in the Serengeti in Tanzania and the Masai Mara in Kenya, where hundreds of thousands of zebras and wildebeest journey together every year.

One thing that zebras like doing is resting their heads on each other when they relax. Like this they can see in all directions, check the area for predators and chase flies out of each other's faces with their tails. They also love dustbathing and rubbing themselves on trees and rocks to get rid of nasty insects.

🐾 Interesting fact: According to research zebras are black with white stripes, not the other way round; and if you'd shave a zebra, it would be all black - it has black skin. ☺

this is the skull of a zebra

zebra hoof prints

Impala
swala pala

One of the most gorgeous looking antelopes on the African planes is the impala. It is very graceful; the males have beautifully sweeping horns, and it has a shiny coat of red and cream with white and black markings.

Impalas are both grazers and browsers, which means they eat grass as well as leaves from bushes and trees - they are so-called "mixed feeders". You can see large impala herds everywhere in East Africa, browsing and grazing in a variety of habitats.

Impalas can jump three meters high and over ten meters far to escape predators. When they run, they are not really fast though, that's why they scatter quickly into all kinds of directions and hide when they are chased.

Impala kids, called fawns, like to play and move together in groups and only go to see their mums when they are hungry. They are just like typical children. :)

a female impala is called a "ewe"

impala tracks

you can see by the ram's horns roughly how old he is

1 year   2 years   2 1/2 years   3-4 years   7 + years

When the male fawns are not even a year old, they get chased out of the herd by older males and start living in bachelor herds. Female impalas start having babies when they are about two years old.

Impalas are always alert as they are the favourite food of many predators.

a male impala is called a "ram"

🐾 Interesting fact: During the mating season, male impalas let out a strange call that sounds like a mix between a grunting pig and a roaring lion.

young rams fighting

Topi
nyamera

Topis, with their long faces, little hump and smooth shiny brown fur with purple patches, are very unique animals. Their coats have a metallic effect when the sun shines on them.

Topis love feeding on fresh green grass. You can find them in open grassland and wooded areas, where they like to rest in the shade of the trees. Topis usually live in small herds, but sometimes you can see hundreds of them together grazing in open areas. They are picky eaters and prefer to only feed on the nice juicy young and soft grass. This is called "selective grazing".

Topis are territorial and defend their territories aggressively. The boss of the herd is usually the dominant male – if he is not around the dominant female will take over his job of defending the herd. When there are intruders, hey hop and jump and run towards them to chase them away.

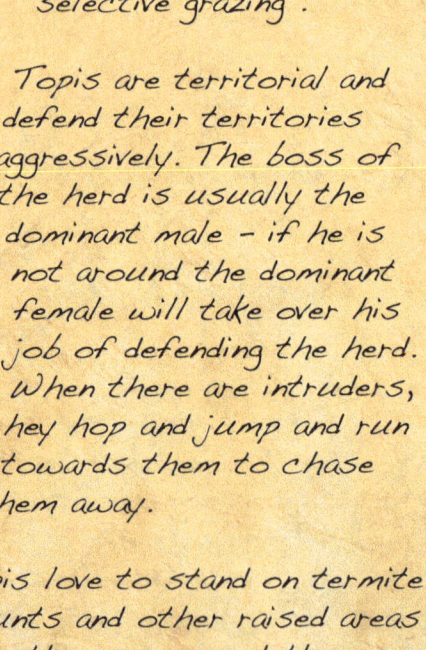

Topis love to stand on termite mounts and other raised areas to view the area around them.

When topis find a muddy place, they often rub their horns and faces in the mud. Researchers think that the mud that clings to their horns is supposed to make them look bigger and scarier.

Once a topi calf is born, it can follow its mother immediately, but the calves often hide from predators in a thicket during the night.

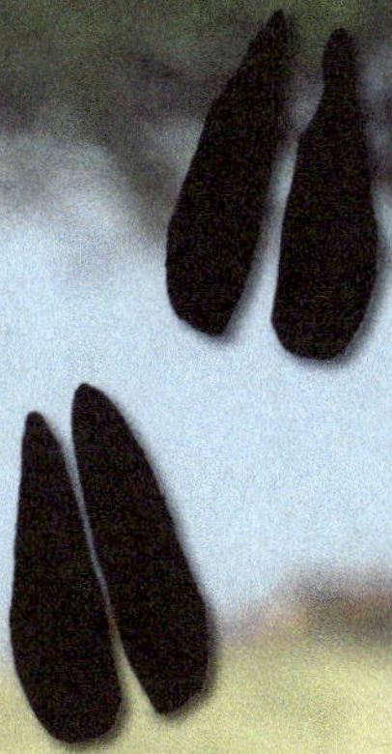

🐾 Interesting fact:
Topis sometimes relax lying down with their mouths resting on the ground – only topis do that.

topi tracks

calves are not born with horns, they grow later

a topi mother with calf

Puku
puku

You can see pukus in East Africa only in a few areas in southern Tanzania. They live mainly in swampy and marshy places and are grazers.

A puku is about the size of an impala, has a shaggy orange coat and only the male has horns. Pukus are crepuscular, which means they are active in the early morning and the late afternoon. During the hot part of the day, they chill out.

Pukus live in small herds of females with their young. In the dry season herds of females often come together for safety.

Dominant adult males are territorial and defend their areas against other males. They try to have as many females as possible stay within their territories, especially during breeding time. After that the males leave the girls and go their own ways again.

pukus fighting

puku tracks

Pukus breed throughout the year. Their babies are pretty clumsy and slow after birth, so as soon as they can, they will hide with the adults in the swampy areas.

Pukus are built strong and sturdy and feel safest when they are in the water, where predators have a hard time following them.

🐾 Interesting fact: When a puku is scared it makes a special shrill loud whistling sound to warn the others.

puku calf nursing

Hartebeest
kongoni

In East Africa you find three different subspecies of hartebeest, the Lichtenstein hartebeest, the Coke's and the very rare Lelwel. Additionally, there is the hirola, or Hunter's harebeest, one of the rarest antelopes in the world, only found in the north of Kenya... despite its name and looks, scientists today think that it actually isn't a hartebeest but a separate species. ☺

The most common are the Coke's and the Lichtenstein hartebeest. The major difference between the two is the shape of their horns. The Lichtenstein hartebeest's horns appear s-shaped from the side - the Coke's hartebeest's horns are formed like a half moon, if you look at them from the front.

The species are otherwise very similar. They have long legs and long faces. Both females and males have horns.

Some people say that hartebeest don't look very elegant, but they are one of the fastest, toughest antelopes on the African plains. The name "hartebeest" is believed to come from the Afrikaans words "harte" (tough) and "beest" (beast).

Lelwel hartebeest

hirola

When hartebeest flee from a predator, they run in one single line, one behind the other, and reach a speed of up to 70 kilometres per hour.

Hartebeest are diurnal grazers, which means they feed on grass in the early morning and evening and rest in the shade when it gets hot.

Like topi they climb termite mounts so they can watch out for danger.

🐾 Interesting fact: The strongest bulls get the best grazing territories – but they must watch out. If they just leave for a drink, they might come back and find another bull has taken over their place.

Coke's hartebeest

Coke's

s-shaped horns

Lichtenstein hartebeest female

male

Lichtenstein hartebeest

hartebeest tracks

Reedbuck
tohe

You can observe three different species of reedbuck in East Africa - the eastern bohor, the common reedbuck and the Chanler's mountain reedbuck.

The smallest of the three is the grey-coloured mountain reedbuck. As the name says they live in the mountains, above 1400m altitude. On a safari you are more likely to see the golden-brown bohor reedbuck or the larger brownish-grey common reedbuck.

Only male reedbuck have horns. The common reedbuck has the longest horns while the bohor's horn tips bend forward the most.

Baby reedbuck stay hidden in the thick grass for a couple of weeks after birth. The mother visits them every day to nurse them, and after about three months the little ones come out of hiding and walk with their mothers.

common male

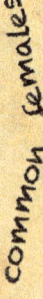

bohor female

bohor males

Both bohor and common reedbuck prefer to live in the long grass, which helps them hide from predators. They also rest there in the hot hours of the day. When they feel threatened, they stand completely still or lie down, trying to blend into the vegetation. Only if a predator comes very close do they run away.

Reedbuck live alone, in pairs or sometimes in loose groups. They feed in the early morning, the late evening and even at night.

🐾 Interesting fact: Reedbuck whistle to communicate with each other.

mountain female

mountain male

reedbuck tracks

Ugandan Kob
kob

The kob antelope looks a bit like an impala, just more bulky - especially the males. Kobs are reddish brown with white rings around their eyes and a white belly and throat patch. The front of their forelegs is black. Males have long sweeping horns with strong ridges.

In East Africa kobs are restricted to parts of Uganda. They graze on open floodplains not far from water as they need to drink every day. Kobs like to feed on grasses and reeds. They are most active during the early morning and late afternoon - they are crepuscular. In the heat of the day, kobs rest in the open grassland.

Although kobs usually live in small herds, they are often seen together in large numbers, where hundreds of animals get together to find water or grazing during the dry season.

Male kobs defend their territories against other males, because only males with an attractive place get chosen by the females for mating. They patrol their territories and "whistle" to show their boundaries. There are certain rituals they use to drive intruders away. If those don't work, they fight against each other, using their horns - they can cause pretty bad injuries.

An advantage of living in open areas is that predators have a hard time approaching them undetected. When they do get attacked, they run into water or reedbeds to escape.

🐾 Interesting fact: The kob is one of only three species of antelope that keep going to the same place to mate – these places are called "leks". The other antelopes that do that are topis and lechwe.

kob tracks

Dik-dik
digidigi

There are four species of dik-dik, three of which you can find in East Africa. The one you'll most likely see is Kirk's dik-dik. In northern Kenya and Uganda you can also come across Guenther's dik-dik. They all look very similar.

Dik-diks are tiny antelopes, hardly bigger than a rabbit, and belong to the dwarf antelopes. They have large black eyes and long hair tufts sticking out between their big ears. Male dik-diks have horns, which are sometimes hard to spot in their funny hairstyles.

Dik-diks are herbivores and eat mainly leaves, young shoots, berries and fruit. They never need to drink; they get all the water they need from their food. Dik-diks feed in the early morning and late afternoon and often rest during the heat of the day in the shade.

The dik-dik's nose looks a bit like a trunk. It has sort of a "cooling system" in it, preventing it from over-heating, even on a very hot day.

cool hairstyle

Dik-diks often live in pairs or small groups in small territories. They mate for life, which means they stay together with the same partner until one of them dies.

Dik-diks like areas which provide them with good cover. You can find them in many places, especially close to dry riverbeds and regions with lots of shrubs.

Dik-dik females can already have babies when they are less than a year old. At birth the baby dik-dik, called "fawn", weighs only as much as a can of soda. The mother hides the fawn in the bush at first, but dik-diks grow up quickly - they are already fully grown at about seven months. Then they have to look after themselves. The father dik-diks chase their sons away and the mothers chase away the daughters; they have to then go find their own territories and mates.

this is the actual size of their tracks

Many predators like to hunt dik-diks, even pythons, baboons and eagles. But these little antelopes have outstanding eyesight and are very fast runners.

Dik-diks mark their territories with their dung, urine and a secretion from the glands at the corner of their eyes. They often pile their own tiny dung balls on top of elephant poo. All strong smells in their territories they try to mask with their own smells.

When there is danger, the male dik-dik whistles and the others go into hiding. Once the danger is over, they all come out and sniff each other's heads. Then they do what they love to do best and mark their territories with their own smells again.

🐾 Interesting fact: Dik-diks are named after the sound of the alarm call the female makes when running away.

Duiker
mindi

If you manage to see a duiker on a safari in Africa, you are very lucky. Duikers are very elusive and shy and love to hide in the forest and thickets. The name duiker means "diver" in Dutch – they probably got that name because they like to dive for cover and hide in thickets.

There are many different species of duiker in East Africa, which differ in size and colour from each other. While the common or bush duiker is usually grey in colour, the red duiker has a chestnut-coloured coat and is much smaller. The smallest is the blue duiker, which weighs only as much as a human baby, while the biggest is the yellow-backed duiker, which can get as heavy as an adult person. There is an extremely rare duiker species called Ader's duiker. It only exists on the islands of Zanzibar, off the Tanzanian coast, and in two locations on the Kenyan coast. The most commonly seen is the bush duiker.

All duikers have a similar build, with the front quarters shorter than the back ones. This hunched posture makes it easy for them to walk through thickets. They look like they crouch down when walking, with their heads held low.

duiker tracks

bush duiker male

red duiker

bush duiker female

When duikers feel threatened, they don't run away. Instead, they crouch or lie down and keep completely still, hoping to blend into the thickets without being seen.

Like many other antelopes, duikers have glands below the eyes. The stuff that comes out of those glands the duikers use to mark their territories. Bush duikers have a tuft of hair growing between their ears, which can look like a horn.

Duiker pairs spend a lot of time grooming each other's heads. It is believed that this helps them to bond.

Duikers feed on leaves, fruit, flowers and tree bark, but they even eat mushrooms, eggs and carrion. Sometimes they catch insects and frogs or even small birds or mice.

🐾 **Interesting fact:** Duikers often follow monkeys around and feed on the fruit that they drop from the trees.

Ader's duiker

blue duiker

yellow-backed duiker

Steenbok
dondoro

You will have to look around very hard if you want to spot a steenbok; they would win a game of hide-and-seek every time. 😊 They are pretty small and if they feel threatened, they hide in the vegetation and put their heads down on the floor with their ears flat. They only run away when danger comes very close. When they do run away they take off like a rocket in zigzag lines and keep stopping along the way to look back or dive back into the bush to hide again. Steenbok also hide their babies for the first few weeks after they are born.

These pretty antelopes have reddish brown coats, very big ears and only the males have horns. Their horns are straight and smooth. Steenbok resemble many other small antelopes, for example oribis, but only steenbok have a distinct black triangle that extends from the nose up to between the eyes.

Steenbok are often found in pairs, although they spend a lot of time apart within the same territory until it is time for breeding. Each pair marks their territory using dung piles.

Steenbok females can already have babies when they are not even a year old. Usually, they have only one baby at a time which weighs not more than about four oranges.

Steenbok are browsers but they also like to dig with their hooves for roots and young shoots of trees and they sometimes eat fruit.

female

steenbok tracks

male

They are often found in open acacia grassland and love areas where the bush has recently been cleared, for example by elephants or people making a road - they probably enjoy the fresh plant shoots that grow in those places.

When it is hot, steenbok feed in the early morning and evening and rest during the day in the shade.

🐾 Interesting fact: Steenbok sometimes hide in aardvark burrows.

Klipspringer
mbuzi mawe

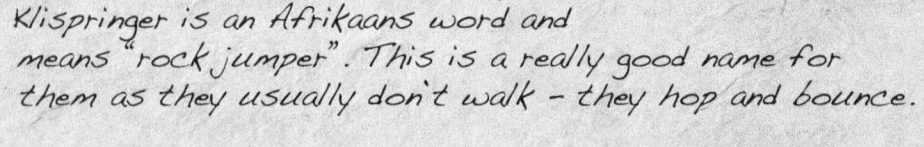

If you come past some "kopjes" (rocky outcrops) be sure to look out for a klipspringer. They have very strong back legs and can jump around the rocks like no other antelope in Africa - their rounded hooves look like a ballerina's feet on her tippytoes.

Klispringer is an Afrikaans word and means "rock jumper". This is a really good name for them as they usually don't walk - they hop and bounce.

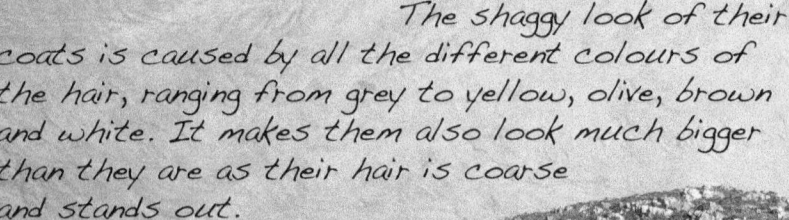

Klipspringer males have small straight horns, but in some parts of East Africa, for unknown reasons, even the females have them.

They are very unique as they are the only antelope in Africa to have hollow hair, which helps them to regulate their body temperature. This is very important as they live on rocks which can get very hot in the sun and cold at night.

The shaggy look of their coats is caused by all the different colours of the hair, ranging from grey to yellow, olive, brown and white. It makes them also look much bigger than they are as their hair is coarse and stands out.

klipspringer tracks

a klipspringer's "ballerina feet"

Klipspringers are very territorial and can get pretty aggressive defending their areas. Both males and females mark the area they live in with a secretion from the glands below their eyes. They rub it on bushes and trees so that other klipspringers can smell where the borders of the territory are.

Klipspringers employ one of their group as a "watchman" who is responsible to look out for any danger. Once a threat is detected the watchman makes a shrill whistling alarm sound to warn the group and they all run for cover.

Klipspringers eat grass, flowers, leaves and fruit.

🐾 Interesting fact: Klipspringers can jump onto and stand with all four legs on a rock the size of the palm of your hand.

Oribi
taja

Oribis have long legs and long necks. The female is a little bit bigger than the male, but only the male has straight spiky horns. Oribis are small antelopes; they weigh only about as much as a two- or three-year-old child.

Oribis like to live in areas with short grass, but they do need a few bushes or patches with long grass to hide in. When they are threatened by predators, they prefer to lie low and only flee at the last second - then they gallop away at high speed. While running, they jump up and down in a distinct rocking-horse gait - no one knows exactly why, possibly to impress or confuse predators. Any ideas?

oribi tracks

Oribis are mainly grazers, but during the dry season they also eat leaves. They love to feed on the young shoots of plants that grow in areas which have been burned by bush fires. Unlike many other antelopes, who get the water they need from the food they eat, oribis need to drink water.

Oribis hide their young after birth in long grass for at least two months. The babies lie completely still so it is very hard to see them. Their mothers come back from time to time to give them milk.

🐾 Interesting fact: The way oribis, and a few other antelopes, jump up into the air with straight legs is called "stotting".

Suni
paa

Sunis are tiny, similar in size to dik-diks. It is difficult to see them on a safari as they are shy forest animals, well camouflaged, and mostly active at night. Even when a predator approaches them, they keep still until the last second - only when danger is very close do they jump up and away.

Since they spend a lot of time in hiding, their main way to "talk" with other sunis is through smell. They have very stinky stuff coming out of large glands below their eyes, which they rub on trees and bushes. The males also use piles of poo to tell other males where their territories are; and they viciously defend them. Only male sunis have horns.

When a suni calf is born, the mother keeps it hidden while she goes out to feed. Sunis eat leaves, flowers, fruit and mushrooms. The calves grow up quickly; they eat the same food as the adults when they are only two months old. At six months old, they can already breed.

🐾 **Interesting fact**: Suni calves are quite heavy when they are born, weighing about 20% of their adult weight. That would be as if a human new-born baby would weigh the same as a two-year old toddler!

suni tracks

Sharpe's Grysbok
tondoro shapi

Grysbok are small antelopes and weigh about as much as two pet cats. They have really big ears and white streaks in their reddish coats and only the males have horns.

Grysbok are nocturnal, very shy, well camouflaged and solitary - so if you see one, you are very lucky.

🐾 **Interesting fact:** The longest horns ever measured on a Sharpe's Grysbok male were a massive 6.3 cm. ☺

grysbok tracks

Lion
simba

lioness carrying her cub

cubs are born with spots which disappear with age

Many people call the lion "the king of the jungle" - but the lion does not really live in the jungle. Lions prefer the open grasslands of the savanna, were they find plenty of prey animals for their dinner and a shady tree for a siesta. Lions spend a lot of time doing nothing - sleeping and just chilling out - about 20 hours per day... imagine that! ☺

The lion is the largest cat living in Africa. The male has a big mane, which usually gets darker with age. The bigger and darker the mane, the more impressive the lion looks. Lions with a thick dark mane are often more successful when fighting other males and when attracting females. A female lion is called a lioness and lionesses do not have a mane.

Unlike most other cats lions are very social. Most of them live in groups of one or two male lions, five or six lionesses and their kids. The group of lions is called "a pride" and the kids of lions are called "cubs". When the male cubs are two or three years old, they have to leave the pride. They then live alone or in pairs until they can find their own pride. Female cubs do the same thing when the pride gets too large.

male — *female*

The lionesses do most of the hard work; they hunt for the pride while the male rests or does the baby sitting of the cubs. It is the male's job to defend his territory and fight off intruders. Lions often steal other predators' prey instead of hunting themselves – so while the lion is not king of the jungle, he is definitely king of the savanna.

When a lioness gives birth to her cubs, she hides them away from the pride. Only when they are about six or eight weeks old does she take them back to the others. They then soon start to play with the other cubs in the pride as well as the adult lions.

🐾 **Interesting fact:** When a lion roars you can hear it over eight kilometres away.

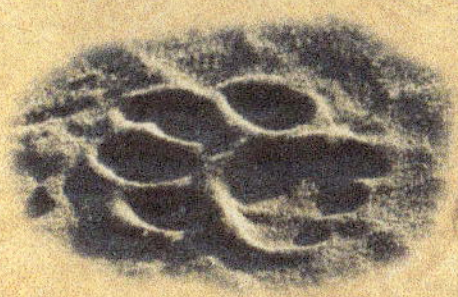

cubs

Lions don't often climb trees – but they can if they want to!

track in the sand

lion tracks

Leopard
chui

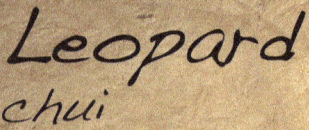

Leopards can be found in many parts of Africa as they can adapt to very different habitats. They live mainly in the savanna as well as in tropical rain forests, preferring thick bush, rocky areas and thickets close to rivers, but they have also been seen on high mountains and close to human settlements.

The spots on the leopard's coat are called "rosettes" and the irregular pattern of those rosettes helps them to blend into their surroundings.

Being so well camouflaged is a big advantage when they hunt; and a leopard is very stealthy when stalking its prey. Leopards eat pretty much any meat they can find – from birds to reptiles, antelopes, warthogs, monkeys and baboons, rodents, rabbits and even fish. They are also happy to eat carrion.

If hyenas or lions find a leopard kill, they will try and steal it. That's why leopards often drag their meal up into a tree to eat it there in peace. Leopards are very good climbers and can easily pull prey, which is even heavier than the leopard itself, up a tree.

Leopards are solitary animals and live and hunt alone. They are territorial and constantly mark their home ranges with claw marks on trees and with pee and poo. Vicious fights between male leopards defending their territories are not uncommon, but even females fight other females off. Males and females often put up with each other in the same area, especially when it is mating time, which is when couples stay together – but only for brief periods of time.

A leopard mother hides her cubs for the first two months after birth to protect them from other predators. From time to time, she gently picks them up by the neck and moves them to a new spot until they are old enough to follow her and to learn how to hunt. Even though the cubs stop suckling when they are three months old, they stay with their mothers for about two years.

Leopards are pretty versatile and sporty – they can swim well, run fast, jump three meters high and over six meters far. Even from the top of huge trees they climb down head first.

🐾 Interesting fact: Leopards can make many noises such as growl, grunt, roar, meow, cough, snarl, hiss and even purr like a pet cat – something lions can't do.

leopard tracks

Cheetah
duma

Cheetahs look a bit like leopards, but they are more slender, have spots instead of rosettes and only cheetahs have black lines called "tear marks" running down their faces from the eyes to their mouths.

While most other cats are nocturnal, cheetahs are active during the day. They spot a gazelle or an antelope, stalk it until they are as close as possible and then sprint to catch it, using their long tails to balance them when taking sharp corners. Since cheetahs don't have sharp claws like other cats - their paws look more like a dog's - they trip and tackle their prey to the ground. Males often hunt in groups while females hunt alone, especially when they have small cubs. They probably need all the meat for their little ones, or maybe they are just better hunters... 😊

As you might already know, the cheetah is the fastest animal on land. It can reach speeds of up to 120 kilometres per hour - that is about three times faster than Usain Bolt. Cheetahs can run that fast only for short periods of time. If they don't catch their prey very quickly, they have to stop and try again another time.

Cheetah males live alone or in groups. They are territorial and they mark their areas by scratching trees or peeing and pooing on plants and rocks. These scent marks work like road and boundary signs for other cheetahs, who can smell "the owner" of the territory and stay away - or pick a fight. When a female, who is ready to mate, is in the area, they pee and poo even more on their boundaries to make sure they show other males who is boss.

cheetah mum with cubs

Sometimes they fight for the girls, but they are usually not too aggressive. Once a cheetah male has mated with a female, he leaves her and she gets to do the rest of the job by herself — unlike lion dads, the cheetah male is not involved in raising or feeding the cubs.

After three months of being pregnant, the cheetah female hides in thick vegetation and usually gives birth to three to five cubs, sometimes more. They are born with their eyes closed and weigh about as much as an orange. After a few weeks they can walk and soon they follow their mothers around. She takes them to new hiding places from time to time as they are very vulnerable when they are so small. The cubs spend most of the time playing with each other and learning how to survive from their mums. They stay with her for more than a year until they know how to hunt by themselves.

🐾 Interesting fact: Cheetahs are easy to tame, and people have kept them as pets and hunting companions for centuries. Unfortunately, cheetahs that are kept in captivity, are usually less healthy and rarely have cubs — so as with most wild animals, it is best to leave them in the wild.

cheetah tracks

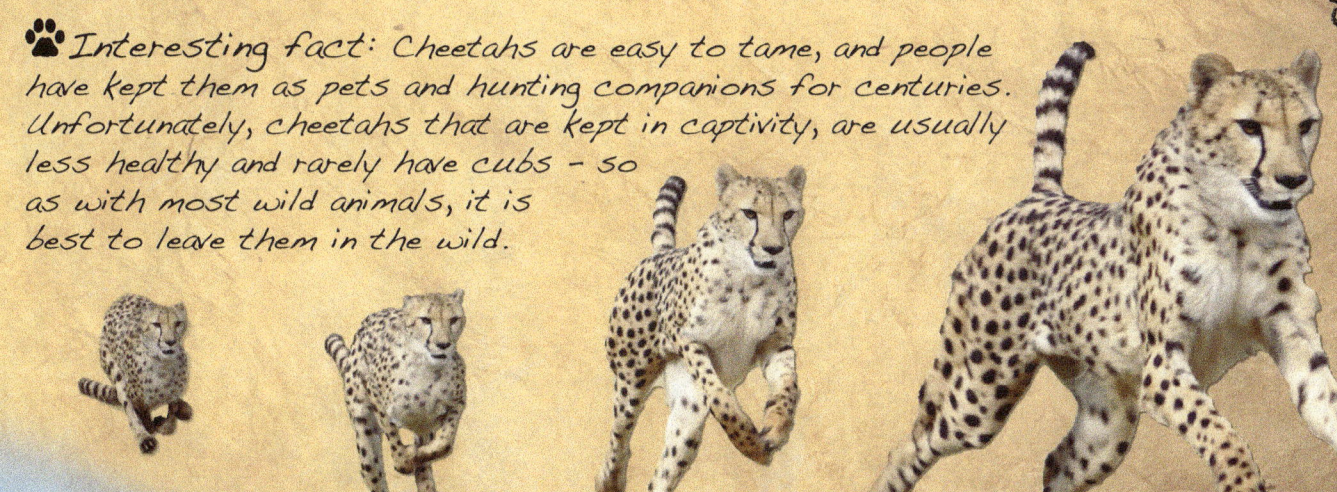

Serval
mondo

Servals are medium-sized cats that can hear, see and smell really well. This helps them to hunt their prey – mainly rodents, but also small reptiles, birds, frogs and even insects. One of their favourite foods are mice. Once a serval has figured out where a rat is hiding, it stalks it quietly and then jumps over two meters into the air and three meters far to bounce onto it – it kills it quickly and swallows it immediately.

Servals are not very social. They live by themselves, except when they are mating and when they have kittens. Serval females give birth to their kittens in thick bush or in dens abandoned by other animals. The mother will stay with her kittens for at least a year or even two – by that time they have learned how to hunt by themselves and are independent.

small head

very long legs

🐾 Interesting fact: Servals even hunt snakes and eat them when they still wiggle.

tracks

Caracal
simba mangu

The caracal is similar in size to the serval but has no spots. It has black tufts of hair on its ears. As caracals are mostly active during the night and very secretive, it is tough to spot them.

Caracals prey on small mammals, birds and reptiles. Just like the serval, the caracal can jump high into the air and knock down a couple of birds at the same time. They even hunt animals which are three times their size.

mother carrying kitten

caracal kitten

The caracal's breeding behaviour is very similar to that of the serval. They also hide their young at birth and kittens are born with their eyes closed – just like pet kittens. Their eyes open when they are about ten days old, and after a month they start to leave their hiding places and play with each other. Even though the kittens start eating meat quite early, it still takes another few months until they have learned to hunt by themselves.

🐾 Interesting fact: Caracals "talk" a lot, they hiss, spit, purr, meow and growl.

tracks

African Wildcat
paka pori

No, this is not a pet cat. It might look just like a tabby, but this is in fact the African wild cat. Pure wild cats are rare today and only found in remote areas as many wild cats breed with domestic cats.

African wild cats have very good ears, which they use to find their prey. They hunt mice, rats, birds, insects and reptiles, usually during the night.

Just like pet cats, wild cats prefer to live by themselves, if it is not mating season. Both males and females are territorial and defend their areas against intruders.

The female gives birth to one to five kittens. They are born blind but after only three weeks, they start hunting with their mother and they leave her when they are about six months old.

wild cat tracks

🐾 **Interesting fact:**
The African wild cat is believed to be the ancestor of our domestic cats. About 10,000 years ago, people started to tame them and some of our pet cats still look just like them today.

African Golden Cat
paka pori

This very rare cat can be found in the tropical rainforests close to the equator. It is hard to spot and can only be seen in very few areas in the eastern parts of Africa - in the west of Uganda, Burundi and Rwanda. The Golden Cat is about twice as big as a pet cat and looks a bit like a caracal but without the tufts on their ears. Not much is known about their behaviour in the wild.

Genet
kanu

The cat-like genet is wide-spread throughout East Africa and the species that are most common are the rusty-spotted genet and the common genet. They look very similar to each other, but the rusty-spotted genet is more grey-yellow in colour, has larger spots and it has no crest on its back.

Genets are omnivores and mainly feed on rodents, small reptiles, insects and birds, with a few eggs, berries, seeds and fruit for dessert.

These animals can live just about anywhere, as long as there is enough food and places for them to hide but they prefer areas with trees and bushes.

Genets are active during the night and sleep in trees in the daytime. Sometimes they live close to human settlements.

Genets are solitary and territorial. They mark their territories using scent, for example by defecating (that's a nice word for "pooing") and urinating (a nice word for "peeing") into so-called "animal latrines", places where they keep going over and over again to "do their business".

common genet

genet tracks about 2cm long

🐾 Interesting fact: You can find wild common genets even in south-western Europe. They were brought in from northern Africa as pets many hundred years ago and made themselves comfortable in the forests of Portugal, Spain and southern France.

Civet
fungo

The cat-like civet resembles the genet in many ways. It looks a bit like a genet, is also nocturnal, lives alone and is an omnivore. Civets are able to kill and eat poisonous snakes, frogs and insects - they must really have very strong stomachs. While genets are normally spotted in trees, look for civets on the ground.

There are two different species of civet in East Africa - the African civet and the African palm civet. The one that is most common is the African civet, which you can recognize best through the black "zorro mask" around its eyes. The spots and bands on its fur are unique like a fingerprint. Civets are very well camouflaged.

The hair on the back of the common civet is longer than the rest of its fur. When the animal feels threatened, it makes the hair stands up to look bigger and scarier. A loud growl adds to the show-off pose.

When civet babies are born in an underground burrow, they can already crawl. After less than three weeks, they leave the nest; they are independent from their mums when they are just two months old.

young civets

🐾 **Interesting fact:** Civets produce smelly stuff in glands on their bums to mark their territories. Somehow people got the idea to use this stuff in perfume. They kept civets in captivity to harvest it - fortunately a similar oil can be produced today in laboratories without using the animals.

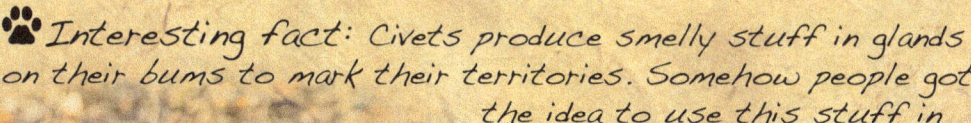

civet tracks

Hyena
fisi

In East Africa you can encounter three different species of hyenas - spotted and striped hyenas as well as aardwolves.

The spotted hyena is the most common as well as the largest hyena species in East Africa - it weighs about as much as an adult woman. Sometimes they are also called "laughing hyenas" as they make a noise that sounds just like naughty laughter. In spotted hyena clans females are the boss. They are also bigger than males and they look after their cubs by themselves.

The striped hyena has beautiful long hair, a thick mane and it is the smallest hyena. Male and female striped hyenas both look after their cubs. They are nocturnal and very shy, so you are lucky if you see one during the day.

The name of the aardwolf means "earth wolf" and it looks a bit like a skinny striped hyena. An adult weighs only about two to three times as much as a pet cat.

aardwolf

striped hyena

spotted hyena
spots fade with age

spotted hyena cubs are born black

Most people think that all hyenas are scavengers. This is not correct – spotted hyenas are good hunters. They have ultra-strong jaws and teeth which can even crack bones. Striped hyenas mainly eat carrion and sometimes fruit and insects. Both striped and spotted hyenas can eat everything other carnivores leave behind – they even digest bone and teeth, which makes their poo look white when it's dry. You'd never guess that aardwolves live off insects, larvae and termites, which they catch with their long sticky tongues during the night.

All hyenas have dens, where they look after their cubs. Aardwolves even have multiple dens within their territories at the same time. They use abandoned burrows made by other animals such as aardvarks or warthogs or they dig their own.

Hyenas have a bad reputation of being smelly, ugly, creepy thieves and there are many legends in which the hyena always plays the bad part. In reality they are intelligent and very important for the balance in nature.

🐾 Interesting fact: An aardwolf can eat 250 000 termites during one night. They never destroy the termite mounds, and they leave enough of them alive to make sure they can come back for a meal another day. 😊

spotted hyena tracks

aardwolf

African Wild Dog
mbwa mwitu

It is very special if you see an African wild dog on a safari as these carnivores are very rare. Another name for the wild dog is "painted hunting dog" - you can easily see why.

Wild dogs prefer to live in the savanna. They are very successful hunters, pursuing mainly antelopes and gazelles as well as hares, porcupines, rodents and birds. The dogs always work in teams, they chase the prey animal until it is exhausted and then start eating it alive. This may sound vicious and cruel, but wild dogs are very interesting and social animals.

In each pack there is one pair of dogs who are boss. The dominant female is the only one in the group who has pups, usually around ten, sometimes more. They are born in an underground den. Everyone in the pack looks after them, not only the mother. While they are small, the adults bring food to the den. Once the pups are a couple of weeks old, the adults take them to their kills and let them feed first while protecting them.

Not many other carnivores behave that way. Healthy adults in the pack may even feed weaker or sick members of the pack. They eat and then regurgitate the food for them, just like they do for the pups of the pack.

wild dog tracks

Sometimes wild dogs dig their own dens, but most of the time they use holes abandoned by warthogs or aardvarks. The pack only stay close to the dens while the pups are small. As soon as they are strong enough, the pack leaves the den, and they migrate great distances on their search for prey.

young wild dog

Wild dogs communicate with each other using many different sounds like whining, sneezing and twittering.

🐾 Interesting fact: Even though they are called "dogs" African wild dogs don't make good pets. People have tried to train them, without success... so best to leave them in the wild.

Bat-eared Fox
mbweha masikio

The name "bat-eared fox" really works well for this small animal - it does have ears like a bat. These large ears are very useful for the small foxes. It might be surprising to you, but they help them to keep cool as they lose a lot of body heat through the big surface of their ears. It is less surprising that the ears help them to hear really well - they work like big satellite dishes.

Bat-eared foxes live in the savanna and other grassy areas. They hide and sleep in dens, which they dig underground. These dens are mazes with many chambers, passages and entrances. The foxes raise their little ones, the kits, in these underground dens.

Bat-eared foxes live in pairs or in small groups of one male with two or three females and their kits, called a clan. Once the kits are born, both parents as well as the clan look after them.

Bat-eared foxes are mainly active in the early morning, late evening and at night. If you see one on a safari you are very fortunate - they are hard to spot.

bat-eared fox tracks

Can you guess what the favourite food of a bat-eared fox is? Termites! The big ears help them locating the little critters, then they scratch and dig for them and lick them up. They also eat beetles, spiders, grasshoppers as well as rodents, scorpions, lizards, eggs and fruit. Bat-eared foxes have more teeth than other foxes (46-50), perfectly suited to chew the tasty insects they love to eat.

termite enlarged

real size termite

fox kit and mum at their den

🐾 Interesting fact: Bat-eared fox kits look a bit like Chihuahua puppies with giant ears. The little foxes are already grown up when they are six months old.

Jackal
mbweha

There are two species of jackal that live in Africa, the side-striped jackal and the black-backed jackal. You might have heard of a third species, called the African golden jackal. Recently researchers have found out that this animal actually has more in common with a wolf than a jackal. This is why the African golden jackal is actually a "new" species and will probably be renamed "African golden wolf" in the future - you'll find him on the next page.

Jackals look a bit like a mix between a dog and a fox; and the two species differ from each other slightly in size, weight and colour.

As the name says, the black-backed jackal has black hair on its back. It likes to live in woodlands and in the open savanna - this is the most common jackal, and you would see one for sure on a safari.

black-backed jackal pup

black-backed jackal

The side-striped jackal is a bit bigger than the black-backed one and has a faint white and a black stripe along its side. This species prefers wetter areas such as scrubs and woodlands.

All jackals are omnivores and will eat whatever they come across. They hunt small animals such as birds, reptiles and small mammals; but they also eat insects, fruit and berries and scavenge other predators' leftovers – even from humans if they have the chance.

Jackals mate for life and both parents look after the pups. The mother feeds them milk for the first few weeks and both parents regurgitate (throw up 🤮) meat for them at the den. When they are about six months old the pups begin to learn how to hunt.

jackal pups

🐾 Interesting fact: Sometimes the pups stay with their parents and help to raise their younger brothers and sisters. They babysit or bring them food.

side-striped jackal

jackal tracks

103

African Golden Wolf
bweha wa mbuga

The African golden wolf is a "new" species. This animal has been around for a long time but it used to be called the "African golden jackal" - people thought it was the African version of the "Eurasian golden jackal". The golden wolf and the Eurasian golden jackal look very similar and behave in similar ways. But now researchers have found out, that the golden wolf is more closely related to coyotes and grey wolves than to jackals. This was possible by doing lots of DNA checks on the different species.

The coat of the golden wolf is a mix of yellowish, grey, silver and white. It likes to live in dry desert and plains areas and is even found in the mountains.

Golden wolves are omnivores, feeding on just about anything they find, from fruit to insects, birds, reptiles and small mammals. They hunt, collect or scavenge their food. When they have too much, they carry it away and hide it for later.

Similar to jackals, golden wolves mate for life and their adult pups often stay with them to help raise their younger siblings.

wolf tracks

🐾 Interesting fact: The African golden wolf is also called a "Serengeti wolf". The Serengeti is a famous National Park in Tanzania.

Honey Badger
nyegere

The honey badger, also called a ratel, is a very unique animal. It is very tough, fierce and strong. If in danger, it may attack much bigger predators like lions or hyenas. The tough skin of the honey badger can even withstand porcupine quills and predator bites.

Honey badgers have big claws which they use to dig burrows or to find food. They feed on lots of different things - berries, roots, bulbs, rodents, lizards, tortoises, insects, snakes, eggs, and birds - and they eat everything, feathers, bones, skin and all.

tracks

One of the honey badger's favourite foods is, you guessed it, honey; the thick skin protects it from the bee stings. Legend has it that a bird called a "honeyguide" leads the badgers to beehives so that they open the hives for them. The badger then feeds on the honey and leaves the grubs for the bird. There is no evidence for this legend, although honeyguides actually do lead humans to beehives.

🐾 Interesting fact: In 2002, the honey badger was listed as "the world's most fearless animal" in the Guinness Book of World Records.

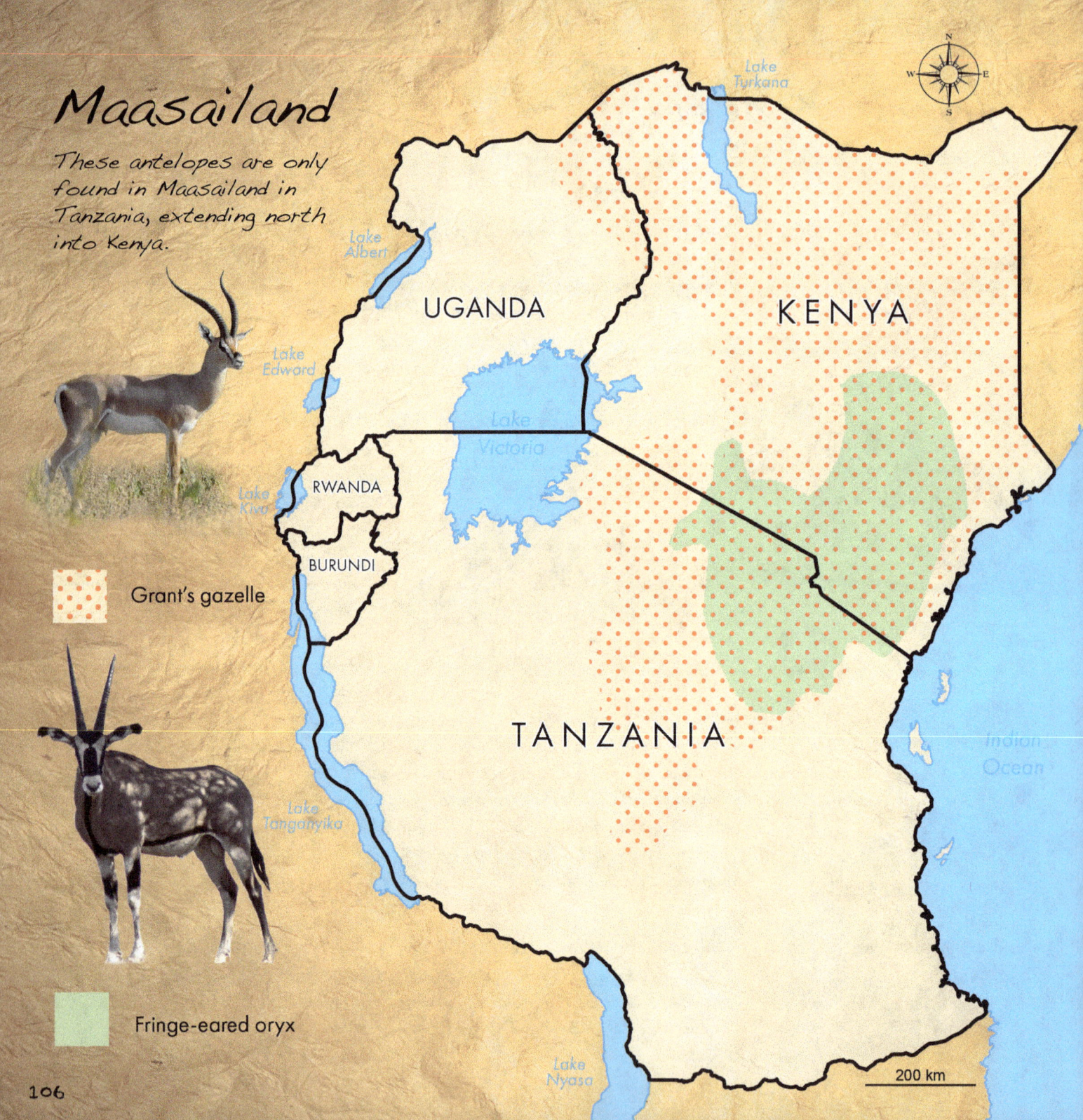

Gerenuk
swala twiga

Gerenuks only occur in East Africa and Ethiopia, in dry thornbush areas. The word "gerenuk" means "giraffe-necked" in the Somali language. The Swahili name "swala twiga" means "giraffe antelope" - a very fitting name for this long-necked animal. Gerenuks have small heads with huge eyes and ears; they are light brown with a darker back, white tummy and white surrounding their eyes. Only the males have horns, they don't use them often for fighting though - unless it is all about a "girl-gerenuk". :)

These strange looking antelopes live by themselves or in small groups. They are territorial and shy and often hard to spot as they blend in well with their habitat. Like many other antelopes, gerenuks have glands next to their eyes which produce some smelly sticky stuff. Male gerenuks mark their areas with this stuff by rubbing it onto branches.

Gerenuks are browsers, feeding on leaves, fruit and flowers from trees and bushes. They can pick leaves and shoots off thorny branches with their pointy mouths without getting hurt.

gerenuk female

gerenuk tracks

108

Gerenuks don't need to drink any water; they get all the moisture they need from their food. The coolest thing is that they can stand up on their hind legs to pull branches down and get to food high in the trees — they are the only antelopes that can stand up like that.

When a female has given birth to her fawn, she hides it in the bush and comes back to feed it a couple of times a day. She also eats all the fawn's poop before the smell can attract any predators.

🐾 Interesting fact: Gerenuk females leave their mothers when they are about a year old, while males stay until they are about one and a half years old.... looks like the boys need a bit longer to grow up.

gerenuk male

Thomson's Gazelle
swala tomi

If you are visiting the Serengeti area of Tanzania and Kenya, you will definitely see many Thomson's gazelles, also called "Tommies". You can find them nowhere else in the wild. Both males and females have horns although the females' horns are much shorter, and very fragile. Sometimes they have no horns at all.

Tommies eat both grass and leaves, depending on the season and on what is available - this makes them so-called "mixed feeders". You often find them together with zebras and antelopes like wildebeest - these are bigger than Tommies and trample and eat all the long grass, which makes it easier for the Tommies to get to the short grass, which they prefer.

Tommy males live by themselves, are territorial and fight other males for their areas, while females and their young live in herds.

Like many other gazelles and antelopes, Tommy females leave their groups to give birth to their fawns. They hide the babies and keep visiting to nurse them. If the fawn gets attacked by a predator that is not too large - for example a baboon - the mother may try to fight it off by headbutting it. When the fawn is about two months old, mother and fawn join the herd together and the fawn starts to eat solid food.

male

tracks

The Tommy is the fifth fastest animal on land in the world. It can run twice as fast as a human athlete, run for longer than most predators and make very sharp turns while running to escape — this is called "stotting" or "pronking". They also do this to alert the others in the herd and confuse the predators following them.

female and fawn

🐾 Interesting fact: Tommy females can give birth twice a year.

East African Oryx
choroa

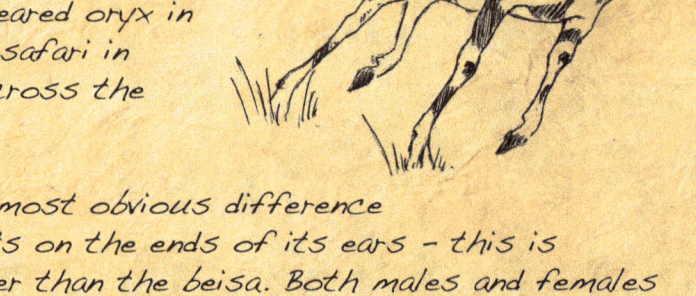

There are two subspecies of the East African oryx, the common beisa oryx, which you can see in northern Kenya, Ethiopia, Somalia and Uganda and the fringe-eared oryx in southern Kenya and northern Tanzania. On a safari in East Africa, you would most likely come across the fringe-eared type.

The two subspecies look very similar. The most obvious difference is that the fringe-eared oryx has black tufts on the ends of its ears - this is where its name comes from - and it is bigger than the beisa. Both males and females have horns, but the female's horns are longer and thinner.

Oryx live in dry grasslands, scrub and woodlands where they mainly eat grass. They absorb most of the water they need from their food and don't need to drink often.

Oryx stay in herds of about 40 animals; most of the herd members are females with calves and young males. Older males often live by themselves.

The animals in the herd challenge each other in different ways to see who is boss within the group. Sometimes they even fight, using their long straight horns, without trying to seriously injure each other.

The herds travel around quite a bit to find food and it is the adult males in the group who decide where everyone is going.

Oryx have a couple of tricks they use to preserve water. They can raise their body temperature which allows them to delay sweating - the less you sweat, the less water you lose. Their pee and poo have very little water in it, only stuff that their bodies can't use. And they have a siesta during the hot midday sun and rather feed in the early mornings - that is also when there is the most moisture in the plants they eat.

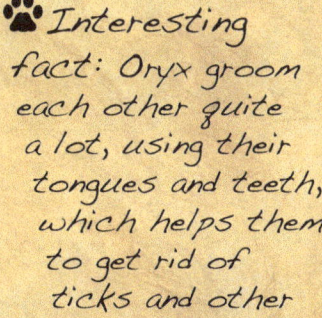
oryx tracks

calf   female   male

🐾 Interesting fact: Oryx groom each other quite a lot, using their tongues and teeth, which helps them to get rid of ticks and other parasites.

113

Grant's Gazelle
swala granti

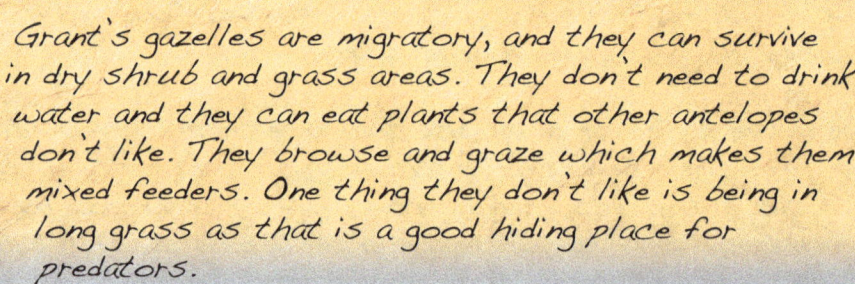

The Grant's gazelle looks a bit like a Tommy, but it is much bigger and has no black stripe along its side. Both males and females have horns. Robert's gazelles are one of five subspecies of the Grant's gazelle and can be found in the Serengeti. They look pretty much the same apart from the shape of their horns, which point outwards.

Grant's gazelles are migratory, and they can survive in dry shrub and grass areas. They don't need to drink water and they can eat plants that other antelopes don't like. They browse and graze which makes them mixed feeders. One thing they don't like is being in long grass as that is a good hiding place for predators.

Grant's gazelle

You can often see Grant's gazelles in the same areas as Tommies, sometimes the herds even mix. Herds of Grant's gazelles come in many different sizes, the herd size depends on the season - the more food is around, the bigger the herd. There are bachelor herds, mixed herds and "harems" with females, young and a dominant male as boss.

Grant's gazelle adult males are territorial, and they have a lot of different ways to show off, for example with macho poses. They do that to let everyone know how strong they are and to threaten intruders in their territories. If all the showing-off does not work, the males will fight each other - especially when it is all about a female. ☺

When giving birth, the Grant's behaviour is similar to a Tommy. They hide their fawns in the bush, keep everything clean by eating all the fawn's poop so predators can't smell them, and come back a few times a day to feed them. Once the little one can walk, they both join the herd together. Since Grant's gazelle females often give birth around the same time of year, there are many other fawns in the herd; they spend their time in peer groups, which are kind of like a kindergarten.

tracks

Robert's gazelle

young male

🐾 **Interesting fact:** Jackals are the main predators of Grant's gazelle fawns. When a fawn is attacked, the mother will try and fight the jackal off with her horns.

115

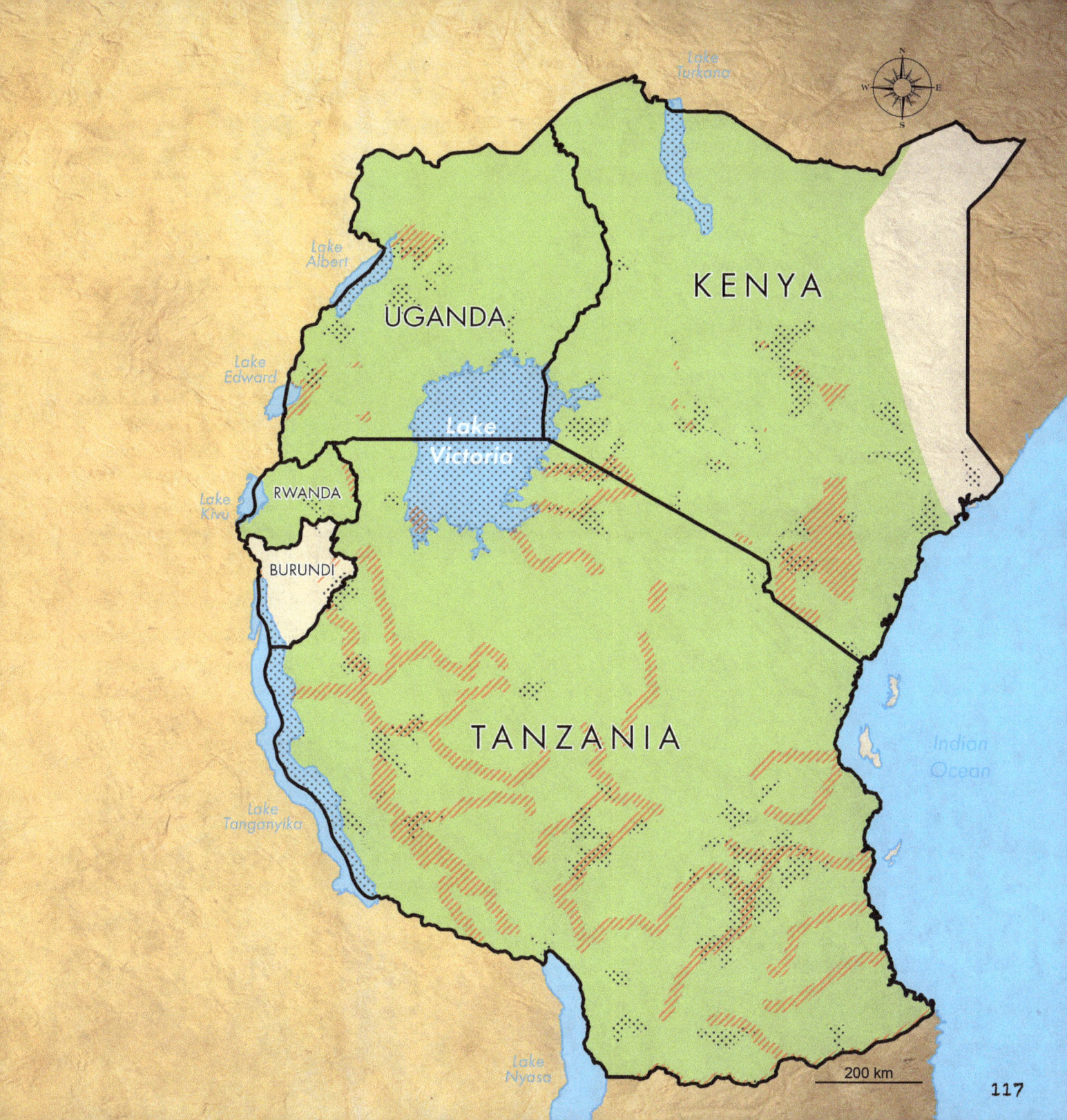

Hippopotamus
kiboko

The hippopotamus, or "hippo", weighs about as much as an average car. Even though it looks so heavy and sluggish, the hippo can run pretty fast and is one of the most aggressive and dangerous animals in Africa.

Hippos live in rivers, lakes and swamps, where they stay cool during the heat of the day. A territorial bull is the boss of his herd, called a pod, of up to 100 females and youngsters. In the evening they leave the water to graze. While they stay together as a herd in the water, everyone does their own thing when they go out at night to feed.

These impressive animals prefer shallow water - they are surprisingly bad swimmers considering that they spend so much time in the water. In deep water, they can sink to the ground and walk or bounce along the bottom - it looks a bit like an astronaut walking on the moon.

Hippos can open their mouths veeeeerrry wide. They don't use their huge front teeth for eating, they pull the grass from the ground only with their lips and then chew it with the molars in the back of their mouths. Hippos often walk long distances at night to graze; they eat up to 70 kilogrammes of grass every day - that is like over 2000 lettuces. :)

hippo pod

back front
hippo tracks

fighting bulls

Hippos do many things in the water; the cows give birth there and the little hippos can suckle underwater. Hippo calves often rest on their mothers' backs when the water is too deep. Hippos can close their nostrils and hold their breath for over five minutes. When they sleep underwater, they automatically bob up and down every couple of minutes to take a breath - without waking up!

Hippo bulls mark their territories with poop that they flick all over the place by wagging their little tails very fast. The resident bull fights aggressively for his place when another bull invades his stretch of water to challenge him. Even though their skin is very thick, they can seriously injure and even kill each other.

🐾 Interesting fact: The skin of hippos can make its own sunscreen. Since it is red, it looks like the hippo is sweating blood, but that is not correct. It is a fluid which is produced underneath their skin and protects them from being sun burnt; it even helps them to fight off some types of bacteria. But it is still important for a hippo to stay in the water during the day, otherwise its skin will dry out.

Nile Crocodile
mamba

You can find crocodiles in lakes, rivers and swampy areas. You might not see them immediately as they often float low in the water with just their eyes and nostrils sticking out. This way they can wait for a long time - even weeks - until an antelope or a bird comes to drink and gets close enough to attack. They grab the animal and drag it under water to drown it. Crocodiles also eat fish and reptiles. When they have their mouths open in the water, a valve closes in the back of their throats so that no water can get into their lungs or stomachs. Crocs can eat as much as half of their body weight in one go, but they can also survive without food for months or even years.

Males are a lot bigger than females and they can grow to over five meters long. Crocodiles have webbed feet, a strong tail and a body streamlined like a speed boat, all of which help them to swim very fast - about four times faster than a person - so better not get into the water with them. Crocodiles can swim without taking a breath for about half an hour. If they don't move, they can stay under water even longer. On land crocodiles can travel pretty fast too, but only for short bursts. ☺

Crocodiles spend a lot of time basking in the sun with their jaws open – the open mouth helps them to regulate their body temperatures. While a crocodile can bite with lot of force, the muscles it uses to open the mouth are very weak. It would be easy for you to hold the mouth of a crocodile shut – if you could get close enough (don't try!!!).

Crocodile babies hatch from eggs. The female digs a hole in the sand not far from the water and lays up to 80 eggs into it, then she covers the nest with sand. She watches over it for about three months until she hears a chirping noise from the nest, then she digs the baby crocs up. The croc mum leads or even carries the little ones to the water where she protects them for a couple of months.

🐾 Interesting fact: It is the temperature in the nest at a certain time which decides whether the baby crocs will be male or female. If the temperature is between 31.7°C and 34.5°C, the babies are males. If it's higher or lower, females are born.

baby hatching

crocodile tracks

Otter
fisi maji

In East Africa, you may see two otter species – the African clawless otter and the spotted-necked otter. They both have waterproof fur, spend most of their time in the water, hunting fish, frogs and crabs or rest in burrows they build in riverbanks. The clawless otter is about three times as heavy as the spotted-necked one.

There are a few differences between these two species, apart from their appearance. Clawless otters are very territorial and live by themselves – unless they want to find a mate or have pups. They mark their territories with smelly "stuff" from their anal glands. Clawless otters prefer waters with trees and bushes for shelter and shade and grass to roll around in to dry themselves. These otters have also been found hunting and foraging at beaches, but they need fresh water close-by.

webbed feet

Most otters have claws and webbed feet. Webbed feet mean that the digits (fingers) are connected by skin, which makes the feet work like paddles – great for swimming. Clawless otters don't have claws on their front feet, that's where their name comes from. They also have less webbing than most other otter species.

spotted-necked otter

clawless otter

clawless otter tracks

Spotted-necked otters are not territorial, live by themselves, but sometimes they hunt together with other otters. They teach their pups how to catch fish by catching one and letting it go for them to try. Pups can swim at eight weeks old.

🐾 Interesting fact: Otters love to play, and pups spend a lot of time swimming, play-fighting and playing with food and rocks. They even catch pebbles that have been tossed in the water, before they hit the bottom.

Vervet monkey
tumbili

If you are lucky enough to go on safari, you will see a lot of vervet monkeys - they are in just about every tree, even close to villages and towns. Vervets are omnivores, but eat mainly fruit, leaves, seeds and flowers. Sometimes they steal eggs from birds' nests or snack on insects. When they live close to humans, they feed on fruit, grains and vegetables found in fields and gardens - they might even climb through a window and take a banana off the kitchen counter.

The vervet female is pregnant for about 165 days - since this is longer than other monkeys, the babies are already more "mature" when they are born.

Vervet babies also grow up quicker. When they are two weeks old, they already start playing with other young monkeys of the troop and at six months old, they eat the same as an adult monkey. They are still very attached to their mums and rely on her for protection and warmth for a long time; but as soon as she has a new baby, the youngster loses his "number one position" with her and becomes a regular member of the troop. When they are about five years old, males leave the group and join neighbouring troops, often where other related males live already. They usually take a brother or buddy with when they move. Females stay with the troop they were born in for life.

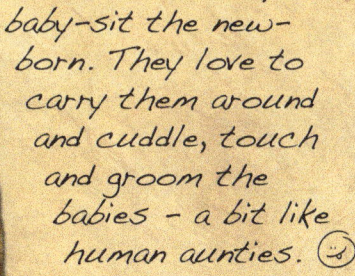
baby

Vervet monkeys use different calls to alert the other members of the troop when there are predators close-by. This way everyone knows immediately if the danger comes for example from a snake, an eagle or a leopard. So, when they hear the "leopard warning call", they head for the trees. When a monkey gives the "eagle warning call", they hide in the bushes. If they come across a dangerous snake, the troop often works together to chase it away. Young monkeys, who don't have enough experience yet, sometimes get it wrong and make the eagle alarm call even if just a harmless bird flies over... ☺ with time they learn how to do it correctly.

🐾 Interesting fact: Already soon after birth, the vervet mother lets other females of the troop baby-sit the new-born. They love to carry them around and cuddle, touch and groom the babies – a bit like human aunties. ☺

vervet tracks

Baboon
nyani

The baboon is one of the largest monkeys in the world and it can look pretty dangerous with its large teeth. In East Africa you'll find two species, the yellow and the olive baboon. The main difference between them is the colour of their fur and olives are more hairy. Baboons spend most of their time on the ground, not in trees like other monkeys.

Baboons are omnivores, eating basically anything - mainly fruit, seeds and other parts of plants, but also insects and rodents. Sometimes they hunt small mammals, even vervet monkeys, or they prey on fish and birds. When they live close to people, baboons often try to steal food from their homes or raid their crops and hunt their sheep.

A group of baboons is called a troop. Baboons are very social animals, there can be up to 250 monkeys in one troop. They sleep together and protect and groom but also fight each other - especially when the boys try to impress the girls in the troop.

Baboons have many ways to communicate. They scream, grunt and make all kinds of noises, you can often hear quite a racket when you see a bunch of baboons.

baboon tracks

They also gesture with their arms and hands, make grimaces and use their entire bodies to express themselves.

Grooming is very important for baboons. It is not just to get rid of ticks and other parasites in their fur, it also strengthens the bonds between them. They often groom each other for hours.

Baby baboons, called infants, hold on to their mothers' fur and get carried around all day long while they are small. When they are a bit bigger, they ride on their mothers' back. The young monkeys play and chase through the trees and come up with all kinds of games. Even adults play with the youngsters, males and females alike. Once the male baby baboons have become adults, they leave the troop and join another one. The females stay with the same troop for life.

🐾 Interesting fact: Baboon babies behave a lot like human children. When they are not happy with something - for example if their mothers refuse to carry them - they scream and jump around, throwing tantrums. 😁

A few more monkeys
nyani wengine

In East Africa there are a bunch of different monkeys to discover, depending on where you may be heading on a safari - here are few examples.

Blue monkeys mainly feed on fruit, but they also eat leaves, flowers and insects. They like to live high up in the shade of tall trees. You can often see them together with red-tailed monkeys. After blue monkey females have given birth, they carry their babies around for the first two months, then they start to let other females watch their babies while they feed alone. Pretty soon the youngsters will follow the others around and play with monkeys of the same age in the troop. Syke's monkeys are a sub-species of blue monkeys.

Red-tailed monkeys have bright orange-red tails and white noses and cheeks. They can collect food in their elastic cheeks, just like a hamster - this way the monkeys don't have to rush their lunch, they can go and eat their "take-aways" in a safe place. When a red-tailed monkey is threatened, it bobs its head up and down or stares at the threat with its mouth open, trying to look scary. To make this look even more impressive, the monkey can pull the skin on its head back by lifting its eyebrows. This way the light colour underneath the eyelids can be seen against the dark fur - this is supposed to be a scary sight for predators... ☺

Zanzibar red colobus

Syke's monkey

With its long white hair and a black coat, the monkey that probably stands out the most is the black and white colobus. Colobus babies are born completely white. Black and white colobus monkeys eat mainly leaves but also seeds, fruit, twigs and flowers.

The black and white's cousin, the red colobus, is very rare. There are a few subspecies of the red colobus, for example the Zanzibar red colobus, which you find – like the name says – on the island of Zanzibar. Just like the black and white colobus, red colobus are vegetarians. They prefer to eat young leaves and they can even feed on some plants which are poisonous for other monkeys.

🐾 Interesting fact: Unlike other monkeys, colobus monkeys don't have thumbs.

Chimpanzee
Sokwe

A chimpanzee is not a monkey, it is an ape. Most monkeys have tails and apes don't. Apes are usually also bigger than monkeys, their bodies are more upright, and their brains are larger. Apes are more closely related to humans than to monkeys - after all, humans are a species of ape too. The chimpanzee is the animal that is most closely related to us.

Chimpanzees, sometimes nicknamed "chimps", can get just about as big and as heavy as people. They live in groups, spend most of their days on the ground and sleep in the trees, where they make a new nest every night in a different place. Each chimp sleeps in its own nest, apart from the youngsters who get to snuggle up with their mothers.

The favourite food of chimps is fruit, but they eat other plant parts too such as roots, buds and leaves. Sometimes they hunt small mammals and collect insects, honey or eggs. One special thing about chimpanzees is that they use and even make simple tools. They use rocks to crack open nuts or squash food into smaller pieces. Some chimps strip leaves and bark off sticks or sharpen them with their teeth. Then they utilise these twigs to "fish" for termites in termite mounds or they dip them into beehives to get honey out. Some chimpanzees crumble up leaves and use them like a sponge to soak up water from hard-to-reach places, then they suck the water out of the leaves. Different groups use different tools and young chimps learn from adults how to use them.

young chimps have light faces

Chimpanzee females are pregnant for about eight months. Once the baby is born it holds on to the mother's belly, but it is still very weak, and the mother has to hold it so that it does not fall. After a few months it is strong enough to ride on the mother's back. It takes a few more years for the babies to stop suckling and become independent, but they stay close to their mothers and are protected by her for still quite a while. Chimpanzee mothers often stay connected to their young for life.

Chimps are very social animals. They communicate with each other in different ways, for example through voice, body language and facial expression. Grooming each other is very important to them. This is not just to get rid of parasites in the fur, it is very relaxing for the chimps – kind of like a spa treatment for humans. ☺

🐾 **Interesting fact:** Chimpanzees know how to use certain plants as medicine when they are sick or injured.

perfect feet for climbing

Gorilla
ekisodde (Luganda language)

Just like chimps, gorillas are apes, not monkeys. The eastern gorillas, which you can find today only in small numbers in Rwanda, Uganda and the Congo, are divided into two subspecies - the mountain gorilla and the eastern lowland gorilla.

Gorillas are mostly herbivores, eating various plants, depending on where they live. They all eat a lot of leaves, but lowland gorillas include more fruit into their diets. These huge apes don't need to drink as their food contains quite a lot of water.

Gorillas usually live in troops of females and their young with an adult male as the boss. If the male has silver-grey hair on his back, he is called a "silverback" - they get the silver hair when they are about 12 years old, along with some large canine teeth. Younger males are called "blackbacks". When a large male stands up on two legs, he is about as tall as a man. They can walk a few meters upright, but normally they move on all fours like chimpanzees.

Gorillas spend most of their time on the ground and not in trees. To sleep they build nests in trees or on the ground. Each has its own nest apart from baby gorillas who sleep with their mothers.

Little baby gorillas are dependent on their mothers for the first few months of their lives - even when they are a year old, they still stay in sight of their mothers all the time.

silverback

Only when they are about six years of age they stop suckling and sleep in their own nests. The male gorillas don't help much in raising the babies, but they do protect them.

Communication using grunts, barks, screams and other sounds is very important for gorillas as they live in dense forests where they often can't see each other; but they also communicate through body signals and facial expressions. The silverback "boss" of the troop is able to emit a certain smell when there is danger - this way he can warn the other gorillas around him without making any noise. He has an impressive way to threaten or intimidate other gorillas. He stands up on two legs, throws leaves around, hits the ground and his chest with his fists and runs around on two or four legs - you can imagine that this display is usually enough to put everyone back in place.

🐾 Interesting fact: The word "gorilla" comes from ancient Greek and means "tribe of hairy women". ☺

front tracks (knuckles)

back tracks

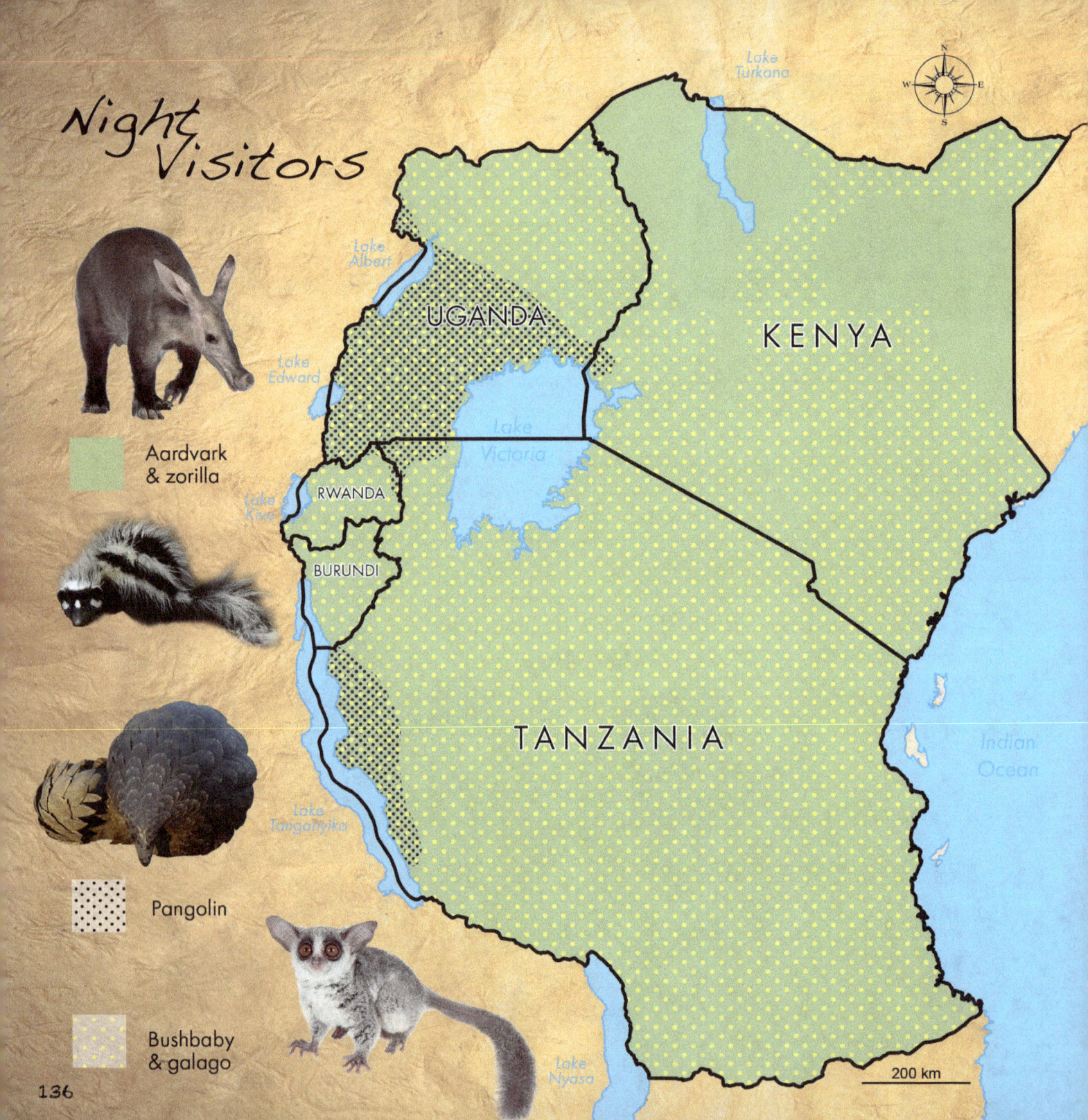

Aardvark
muhanga

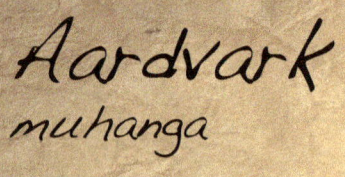

The name "aardvark" is Afrikaans and means "earth pig" - this name is pretty suitable. Aardvarks spend a lot of time digging and they rest underground during the day. They use their strong legs and sharp claws to dig burrows or to break open termite mounds and ant hills - they do that as the only food they eat is ants and termites. Once they find them, using their super good ears, they snatch them up with their very long sticky tongues.

Even though the aardvark looks a bit like a giant mouse, weighs as much as an average adult person and is taller than a Labrador dog. Aardvarks have one cub at a time, which is born with wrinkly skin and floppy ears. After few weeks, the little varks have hair, the ears are up, and they go termite hunting with their mums.

a it tracks

🐾 **Interesting fact:**
Aardvarks have many ways to defend themselves - they run away, lie on their backs and kick, or they quickly dig a hole to hide. They are one of the fastest diggers in the world.

Pangolin
kakakuona

Just like aardvarks, pangolins catch ants and termites with their long tongues and chill out in burrows during the heat of the day. Pangolins can close their noses and ears so that no insects get in there while they feed.

Pangolins are covered in scales, which protect them like a knight's armour. The scales are made out of the same material as your fingernails, but they are very strong. Baby pangolins' scales are soft but they get really hard as they get older. When pangolins are threatened, they curl up into a ball to protect the vulnerable underparts of their bodies. They can slash their attackers by thrashing their tails around and by moving their scales in a scissor-like way.

🐾 Interesting fact: When pangolins want to move with a bit of speed, they walk on their back legs - just like a T-Rex dinosaur.

back track   front track

Hedgehog
kalunguyeye

The African pygmy hedgehog is also called a four-toed hedgehog because it has only four toes on its hind feet. They only weigh about as much as a kitten.

Hedgehogs are nocturnal and solitary, moving around large areas at night to find food. They like to eat grubs, spiders, worms, snails and insects as well as small mammals and reptiles and a few plants. Even venomous snakes and poisonous scorpions are sometimes on the menu – they are pretty tough little animals.

When a hedgehog is attacked, it curls up into a prickly ball – this way it protects its head and legs. The spines stick out and the hedgehog tries to jab the attacker. They even sleep in this curled-up position and it would be very hard to pry them open.

When baby hedgehogs, called pups, are born, they are tiny, blind and completely helpless, but after about six weeks, they are ready to leave their mothers.

Interesting fact: Hedgehog pups are covered in a membrane when they are born, so that they don't hurt their mother with their spines.

tracks

Porcupine
nungunungu

A porcupine is a rodent, feeding mainly on fruit, berries, roots and bark, usually at night. If they have the chance, they will also raid crops, planted by humans.

African brush-tailed porcupine

Porcupines defend themselves against predators using their sharp quills, just like hedgehogs; but they have some additional ways of scaring their attackers off. They can make a noise by clattering with their teeth, stomping their feet and rattling their quills, and they give off an unpleasant smell. Porcupines will also ram sideways or backwards into attackers or swing their tails at them. They can inflict serious injury that way. Unlike hedgehogs, porcupines lose their quills - they get stuck in the attacker's flesh or mouth and it is very difficult to get them out. Even lions have respect for porcupines. ☺

Cape porcupine

Porcupines mate for life and live in colonies with their young in a range of underground burrows. The pair defends their territory together against intruders.

tracks

🐾 Interesting fact: Porcupines can regrow lost quills.

quills

Zorilla & African Striped Weasel
kicheche & kicheche nyoka

The zorilla, also called a striped polecat or African skunk, is a small, but pretty aggressive animal. Zorillas are very territorial, they mark their territories with poo and some smelly secretion from glands on their bums. They also spray this stuff at predators' eyes - it burns and makes them blind for a while.

Zorrilas have a wide variety of calls, screams, growls and signals which they use to communicate with each other or to scare off predators.

The African striped weasel looks similar to the zorilla, but it is less than half its size - it only weighs about as much as a mango. It too can spray smelly stuff to defend itself.

Both of them are solitary carnivores, hunting small reptiles, rodents, birds and insects at night. Striped weasels even kill rodents as big as themselves.

If you are lucky enough to see one of them, don't go too close... they really do stink.

🐾 Interesting fact: The name "zorilla" comes from the Spanish word "zorro" which means "fox". The babies of the striped weasel at birth weigh weigh only as much as a teaspoon of sugar.

Bushbaby & Galago
komba

Bushbabies and galagos are two different names for members of the same family of animals. The name bushbaby comes either from their cute look or from the baby-like sound of their cries at night. In the Afrikaans language, they are called "nagapies", meaning "night monkeys".

Bushbabies are primates, just like monkeys and apes. They come in different sizes, the smallest weigh as much as a small apple, the largest over 13 times that amount.

Bushbabies are nocturnal. All of them have giant round eyes, which help them to see in the dark. They also have excellent hearing, with big ears like radar dishes - perfect for tracking down insects. The ears can be folded to protect them while they sleep or jump.

Bushbabies spend most of their time in trees, hunting for small animals and insects or feeding on fruit. They also lick gum, a sap oozing from certain trees.

Their long tails help them to balance when leaping from tree to tree - they have very strong leg muscles. Bushbabies are very fast and can even snatch insects out of the air while jumping.

thick-tailed galago

Northern greater galago

lesser bushbaby

🐾 Interesting fact:
Bushbabies pee on their hands and feet to get a better grip.

Senegal bushbaby

Pigs

■ Bushpig

there are common and desert warthogs in East Africa
they look similar

▨ Warthog

smallest wild pig in Africa

■ Red river hog

biggest wild pig in the world

▦ Giant forest hog

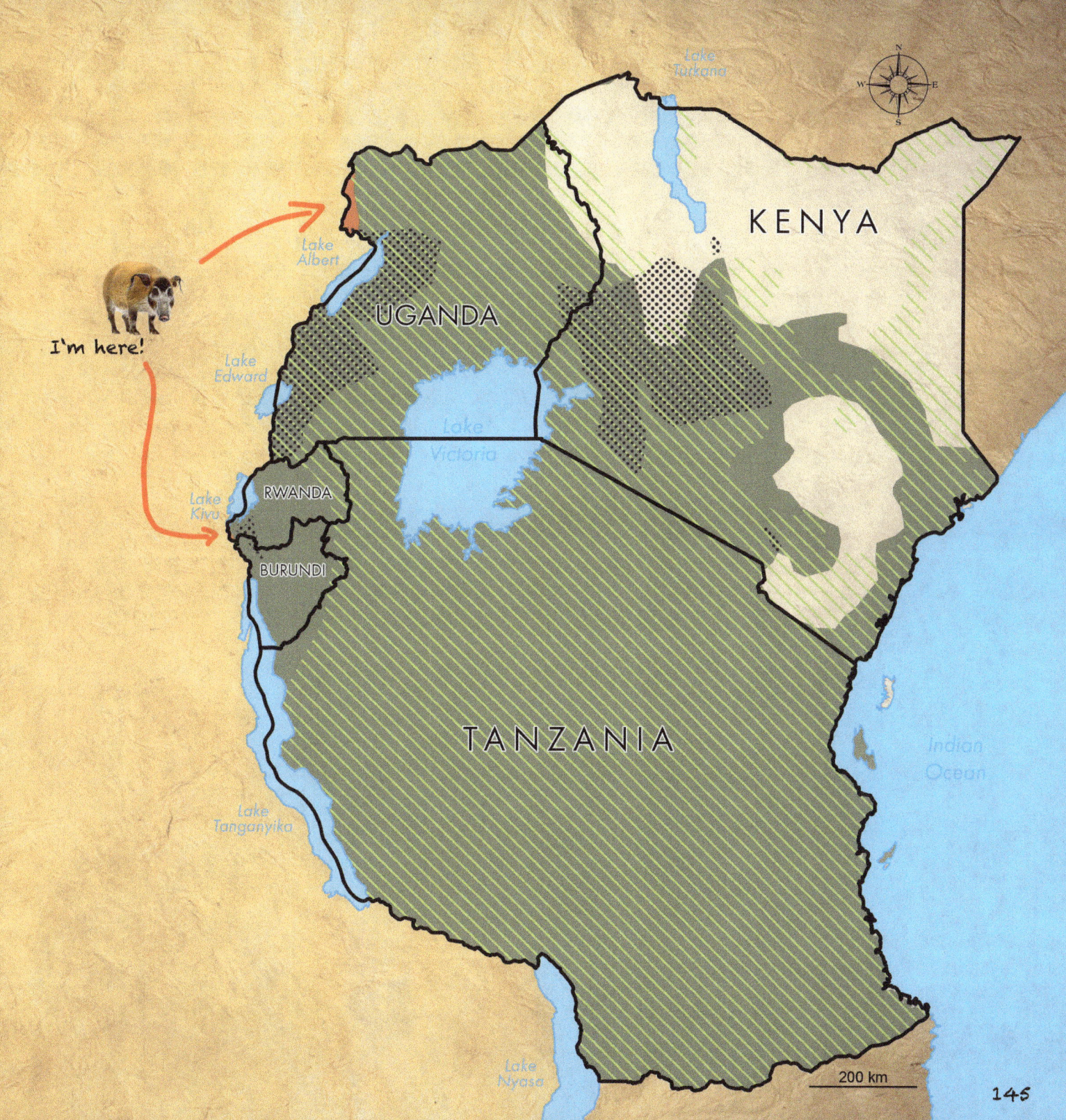

Bushpig
nguruwe

Bushpigs like to live in groups of up to twelve. A group of wild pigs is called a "sounder". There are usually a male and a female who are boss in the sounder, living together with a few females and youngsters.

Bushpigs are omnivores, feeding on anything from roots to fruit, insects, bulbs as well as carrion. If they get the chance, they will raid a farmer's potato, maize or vegetable field. Sometimes they follow monkeys around to catch the fruit they accidentally drop while feeding in the trees.

The male leader of the sounder breeds with multiple females (male pigs are called boars). When the female pig, the sow, has piglets, their father helps raising them. At the age of six months, the piglets are already independent.

Bushpigs are very territorial and can get very aggressive when they want to defend their territory or their piglets. They are strong and have razor-sharp tusks.

Bushpigs love to wallow in water, mud and dust. This helps them to cool down and to protect their skin from insects.

Interesting fact: On rainy or cold days, bushpigs build nests to stay warm.

Warthog
ngiri

Warthogs have long tusks sticking out of their jaws – a long pair on the top and a short pair on the bottom. The bottom tusks get very sharp because they rub against the top ones when the pig opens and closes its mouth – and they can be very dangerous. Warthogs use their tusks to defend themselves against predators, fight other warthogs or for digging. The warts on the side of the face, which give them their name, protect them when fighting. Especially the males have large warts.

Warthogs feed mainly on grass but also eat fruit, bulbs or berries. Sometimes they eat worms or carrion. Although they don't need to drink, they happily do if water is close by.

Instead of digging their own holes, warthogs often steal the burrows from other animals. The warthog babies, called piglets, get to go in first, then the mother follows them backwards so that she can see danger at any time and block the entrance. Warthog mums may even attack predators to defend their young.

🐾 Interesting fact: Warthogs "kneel down" with their front legs while feeding and rest on their knees, which are covered with thick skin.

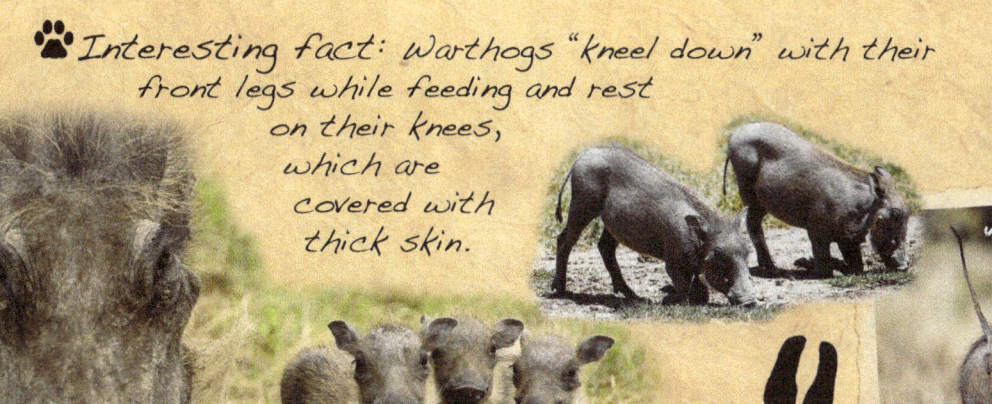

warthogs run with their tails up – why? No idea...

Giant Forest Hog
nguruwe

As you can guess from the name, giant forest hogs are pretty big. In fact, they are the biggest wild pigs in the world and one can weigh up to three times as much as an average adult man. They like to live in forested areas in sounders (groups) of up to 20.

When a female is ready to give birth, she leaves her group and builds a big nest out of branches and grass. After giving birth she stays there with the new-borns for a few days before returning with them to the sounder. The little piglets are then protected by all members of the group – the male leaders can get very aggressive, even attacking predators if they see their sounder threatened.

🐾 **Interesting fact:** Giant forest hog piglets can nurse from any female in the group, not just their own mothers.

Red River Hog
nguruwe

teenage hogs, about a year old →

adult, older than two ↓

← piglet, under six months old

As you can see on the map at the beginning of the chapter, there are not many places in East Africa where you can get to see a red river hog... but they look pretty cool, and they are interesting animals, so they'll get their own page in this book anyway. ☺

Red river hogs have a similar diet to bushpigs - they eat just about anything they come across and even hunt small mammals, insects and reptiles. The hogs use their snout, tusks and front feet to dig for roots and tubers, mostly at night.

These hogs live in sounders (groups) of up to 20. While they are very social animals, they try to stay away from other groups and when they happen to meet, they threaten each other - they might even get into fights. They can fluff out the hair on their faces to make themselves look bigger and appear more dangerous.

Red river hogs love to wallow in water, and they are good swimmers. They can run fast and have a variety of grunts and squeals to communicate with each other.

🐾 **Interesting fact:** Red river hogs sometimes follow chimpanzees to collect the fruit that they accidentally drop when feeding in the trees.

Hyrax
pimbi

Hyraxes, also called dassies, look like giant tailless rats or overgrown guinea pigs, but they are not related to them, and they are not even rodents. There are rock hyraxes (also called bush hyraxes) and tree hyraxes; all are herbivores, but their behaviours differ.

Rock hyraxes live, as the name says, on rocky outcrops. Their feet are padded and sweaty, helping them to scoot around on the rocks. Their bodies are not adjusted to regulate heat well, so they spend a lot of time sun-bathing to get warm. On cold and rainy days, they might not even get up and rather stay in their burrows, huddled up with other hyraxes, only going out when the sun is up. 95% of their time they spend resting.

Tree hyraxes are great climbers. They are nocturnal. If you hear a shrill call, that is getting louder and louder during the night, it is probably a male tree hyrax, announcing his territory.

🐾 Interesting fact: Surprisingly, hyraxes are the closest relatives of elephants.

Mongoose
nguchiro

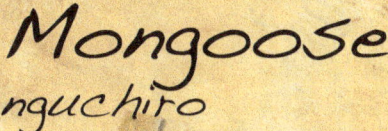

slender mongoose

dwarf mongoose

Mongooses are little mammals that look a bit like squirrels. There are a bunch of different mongoose species in East Africa. The smallest, the dwarf mongoose, weighs only about as much as a grapefruit. The heaviest, the white-tailed mongoose, weighs up to 20 times more.

Mongooses are carnivores and hunt frogs, insects, rodents, lizards, birds, worms and feed on eggs and carrion - depending on the species and where they live. Some mongooses know how to break open eggs by picking them up and throwing them on a rock to crack them open.

A mongoose that is very common in East Africa is the banded Mongoose. They live in large groups and have their pups in underground burrows.

white-tailed mongoose

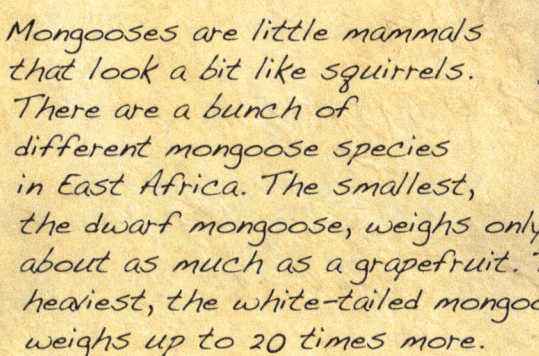
dwarf mongoose

banded mongoose

🐾 **Interesting fact:** Some mongooses are immune to poisonous snake bites.

Mole, Shrew, Gerbil, Mouse & Rat
fuko, kirukanjia & panya

Ok, so you think mice and rats are yucky animals? Not true. They are an important part of the ecosystem, not only in Africa. There are hundreds of species of mice, rats, shrews and moles living in East Africa and they have the coolest names. Here are a few examples, no kidding, they all do exist: Long-eared flying mouse, African demon mole rat, Tiny fat mouse, Fiery spiny mouse, Yellow-spotted brush-furred rat, Delicate mouse, African groove-toothed rat, Hildegarde's broad-headed mouse, Moonshine shrew, and Turbo shrew.

Moles are animals that are highly adapted to their underground lifestyle. They have forepaws like shovels to dig their burrows. Their eyes and ears are tiny as seeing and hearing is not of much use if you live in the earth. Moles feed on earthworms and other invertebrates in the tunnels they dig – they can sense the vibrations the prey animals make.

The moles you can find in East Africa – for example the Golden Mole – are not "true" moles, as those live in North America, Europe and Asia. The moles in Africa are not related to "true" moles, but they have independently developed to look and behave in similar ways.

African pygmy doormouse

Mice, rats and gerbils are rodents – rodents have a pair of incisors in the top jaw and a pair in the bottom jaw, which keep growing throughout their lives. Incisors are the teeth that are in the front of the jaws and are used to gnaw. By the way, humans also have incisors, eight of them... but we are not rodents, because ours don't keep growing.

Rats are usually bigger than mice and have a shorter tail in comparison to their body size. Gerbils live in very dry places, like deserts.

golden-rumped elephant shrew

Four-striped grass rat

elephant shrew

Shrews look like tiny mice with a longer nose, but they are not rodents. They are more closely related to hedgehogs and moles.

Shrews have one set of teeth that has to last them a lifetime - weirdly, they lose their milk teeth before birth. Shrews feed on seeds, insects, worms and nuts.

The elephant shrew is actually not a shrew, even though it looks like one. Believe it or not, elephant shrews are actually more closely related to an elephant than to other shrews. That's why some researchers suggest a change of name to "Sengi", their name in many African languages.

The naked mole-rat is a very special rodent. It is the longest living rodent and can live over 30 years, while a mouse only lives around three years. They live underground in dry grassland areas and their bodies are adjusted to the lack of oxygen in their tunnels. This is one of only two known mammals living in colonies similar to ants, with one queen and a few males for reproduction. The other mole-rats in the community are worker rats, who maintain the tunnels and collect food, and soldiers who defend the burrows. The tunnel systems can stretch up to five kilometres long and an average of 80 mole-rats live in one colony.

naked mole-rat
life size

acacia tree rat

🐾 Interesting fact: The naked mole-rat is also called "sand puppy".

Squirrel
chindi

There are many different species of squirrel in East Africa, and they come in all kinds of colours and sizes. Some live in forests and can glide from tree to tree, others prefer to be on the ground and live in burrows.

Squirrels feed on nuts and seeds and some of them add eggs, insects, flowers, bark and fruit to their menu - or they get "take-aways" by stealing farmers' crops. ☺

Some squirrels are endemic to East Africa, which means you can only find them there. Swynnerton's bush squirrel, for example, is endemic to Tanzania and you can find it on forested mountain slopes, like on Mount Kilimanjaro.

Lord Derby's scaly-tailed squirrels can glide from tree to tree over distances as far as 250 meters - that is two and a half times as long as a football field. Their bodies are built in a way that they look like paragliders when they stretch their legs out.

squirrel in "flight"

🐾 **Interesting fact:** The word squirrel comes from the Greek words "skia", meaning "shadow", and "oura", meaning "tail" shadow tail. They can use their tails for balance and like a parachute when falling.

Hare & Rabbit
sungura

Rabbits are normally smaller than hares, with shorter hind legs and shorter ears; they make their nests underground while hares have their nests above ground. Rabbits are rare in Africa so most bunnies you will see on a safari are hares.

The hares in East Africa are nocturnal, hiding in the daytime in long grass, rocks or thickets.

They feed on grass and flowers, and they eat their own poo... this way their food basically goes through their stomachs twice and they can get more nutrients and minerals out of it. ☺

Hares can run very fast, and they make sharp turns when they are fleeing from a predator.

Their large ears are full of blood vessels which help to regulate their body temperatures.

African savanna hare

Cape hare

🐾 **Interesting fact:** Despite its name, the East African Springhare is in fact not related to hares. It is a rodent and looks more like a cross between a kangaroo and a rabbit.

springhare

Some scaly creatures

■ Tortoise, Lizard, Chameleon & Snake

Terrapin - wherever you find water (except the ocean)

■ Sea snake

■ Sea turtle

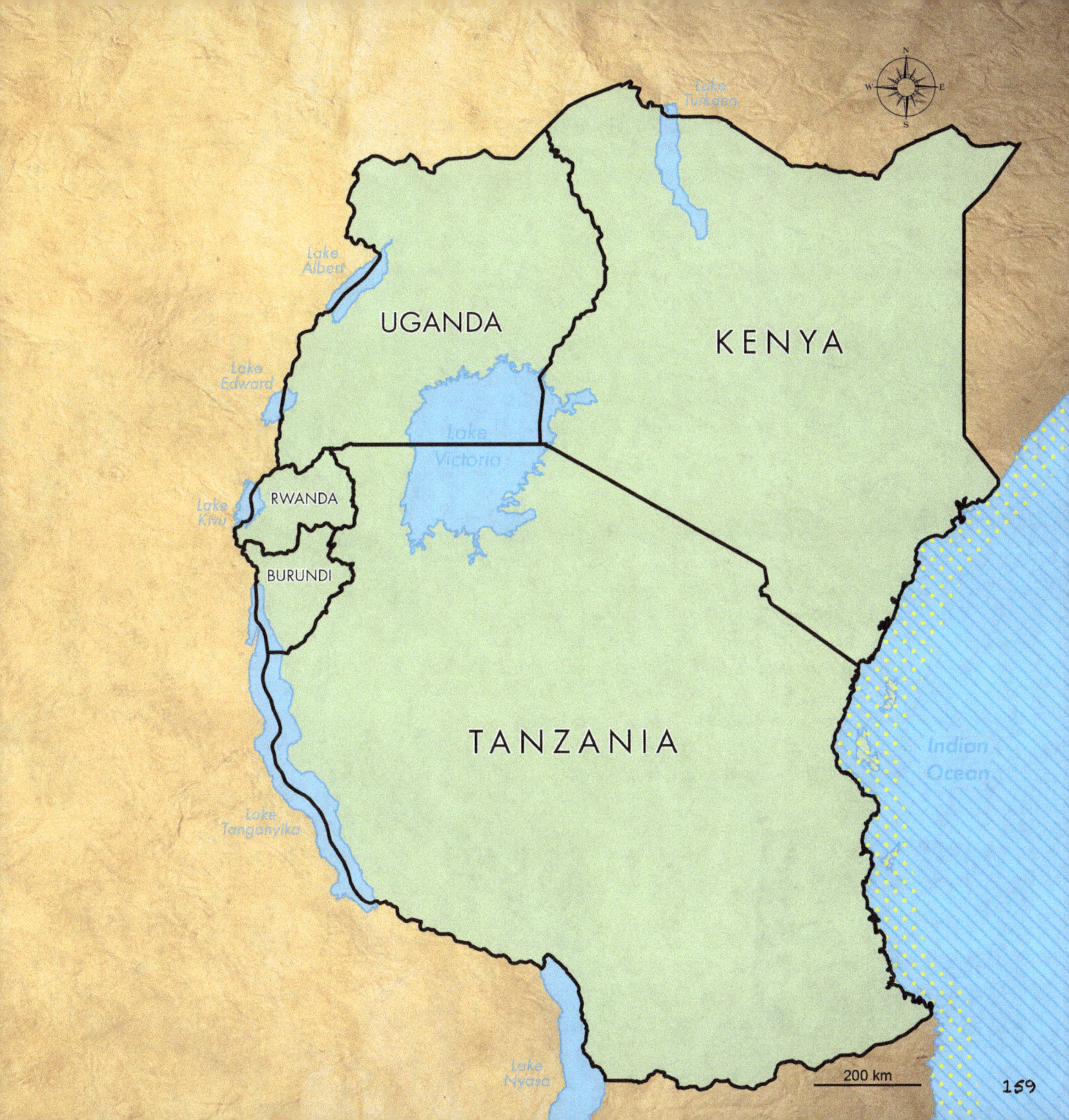

Lizard & Chameleon
mjusi & kinyonga

You can see so many different shapes and sizes of lizards in East Africa. Chameleons, skinks and geckos are all lizards too. They are carnivores, catching insects with their tongues. Some of them also nibble on fruit and flowers.

Lizards are reptiles. They are cold-blooded which means that their body temperature is dependent on the environment. They need the sun to warm up and a shady spot to cool down.

Chameleons are really cool lizards - they can move their eyes independently from each other and look into different directions at the same time. Some of them can change the colour of their skin. Scientists think that they do that to communicate with other chameleons, for example when they want to impress females. They also get darker when they are cold as darker colours absorb more heat. Many people think that they change their colour to camouflage

themselves, but they don't really need to do that as they can move fast when they are in danger.

The monitor lizard, also called a leguan, can be over two meters long.

Skinks usually have very short legs and not much of a visible neck. There are hundreds of different species of skinks all over the world.

Skinks and geckos can get rid of their tails when a predator grabs them and then grow them back.

You will often find geckos scooting up and down the walls inside homes in East Africa. No reason to be scared of them – they are harmless, and they eat all the insects in the house. Most people like them around.

🐾 Interesting fact: Most lizards have eye lids and can blink. Geckos can't so they lick their eyes to keep them clean and moist.

Fischer's chameleon

monitor lizard

Taita blade-horned chameleon

gecko

helmeted chameleon

African striped skink

agama female

green keel-bellied lizard

Tortoise, Terrapin & Turtle
kobe

Depending on where you are coming from, the meaning of the terms turtle, terrapin and tortoise are different. In some languages there is only one word for all three. In North America, all of them are called "turtle" and "tortoises" are defined as "slow moving turtles that live on land". Some English names use different terms for the same animal - for example the "variable hinged terrapin" is also called "variable mud turtle". Confusing, isn't it?

Everyone might not agree 100%, but below is how I seperated them in Africa - I think it makes things easier. :)

green turtle — right after hatching

Turtles spend most of their time in the water, mostly in the ocean. Their legs are more like flippers and their bodies are streamlined and perfect for swimming. They only come out of the sea to lay their eggs.

Tortoises live on land, they have rounder shells, and they are the longest-living animals in the world - between 80 and 150 years.

- Terrapins spend time in the water and on land. Animals that do that are called "semi-aquatic". Terrapins often have long claws on their feet, which allow them to climb out of the water. You find terrapins in freshwater lakes, rivers and brackish waters.

Tortoises, turtles and terrapins lay eggs in soil or sand. The female carefully chooses the

terrapin sunbathing on hippo

loggerhead turtle

leopard tortoise

spot to be sure that it is sunny and that there is no risk of flooding. Then she digs a hole, lays her eggs in it and closes it again with soil or sand so it becomes invisible. That's the mother's job done. The little ones hatch after six to ten weeks and dig themselves out of the hole - this might take them as long as a week to accomplish.

Terrapins, some turtles and some tortoises are omnivores (everything-eaters), feeding on various plants and fruit, insects, worms or little fish and jellyfish, depending on where they live. Most tortoises and some turtles are herbivores (plant-eaters) - green sea turtles, for example, don't eat meat, they prefer algae. Baby turtles need a lot of protein, so they have mainly carnivorous (they eat meat) diets while they grow up. Loggerhead turtles eat just about anything, including their own babies... ☺

🐾 Interesting fact: Just like crocs, the sex of the turtle hatchlings depends on the temperature in their nest. If it is warmer than a certain temperature, there are more girls, if it is colder, there are more boys.

green sea turtle

Snake
nyoka

Many people don't like snakes, but they are really fascinating reptiles. It is a myth that they are slimy, as their skin actually feels dry to the touch.

Snakes only bite people when they are hurt or feel threatened and even then, they often don't inject any venom – this is called "dry biting".

Snakes can sense vibrations on the ground and slither away when people approach. There are some snakes however, that rely on their camouflage and don't move out of the way. Instead, they stay very still and hope you don't see them. If you come too close, they might strike out. Puffadders are snakes that do that.

All snakes are carnivores, eating small animals, fish, eggs and insects. They swallow their prey whole as they can't chew. The size of the prey depends on the size of the snake. Pythons can swallow entire antelopes.

It can take days for snakes to digest their food and then they may not have to eat for weeks.

Not all snakes are venomous. Pythons for example, kill their prey by constriction – they wrap their bodies around the victim and squeeze it until it suffocates.

puffadder

yellow-bellied sea snake

Snakes can smell with their forked tongues; they keep flicking them to "taste" the air.

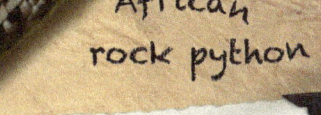
African rock python

Most snakes lay eggs and leave them to hatch by themselves. Some snake species however, stay close to the eggs until the babies hatch. Pythons even look after their little ones until they are a week or two old, and protect them from predators. Sea snakes, which live in the ocean, don't lay eggs, they give birth to live snakes.

The tails of sea snakes look like paddles, which helps them to move through the water. They can stay for hours under water, then they need to swim to the surface to breathe - this is also where they drink fresh rainwater before it mixes with the salty sea water. Most sea snakes are venomous.

very dangerous

black mamba

Green mamba

Snakes shed their skins from time to time. You might find very thin pieces of that skin on the ground. You might even be able to identify which snake left it there by looking at the pattern of the scales.

🐾 Interesting fact: Snakes have eye lids that are always closed - thankfully they are transparent so the snake can see. They are called "brille" which is German for "glasses".

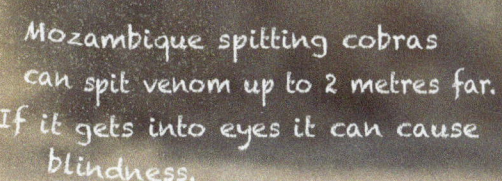

Mozambique spitting cobras can spit venom up to 2 metres far. If it gets into eyes it can cause blindness.

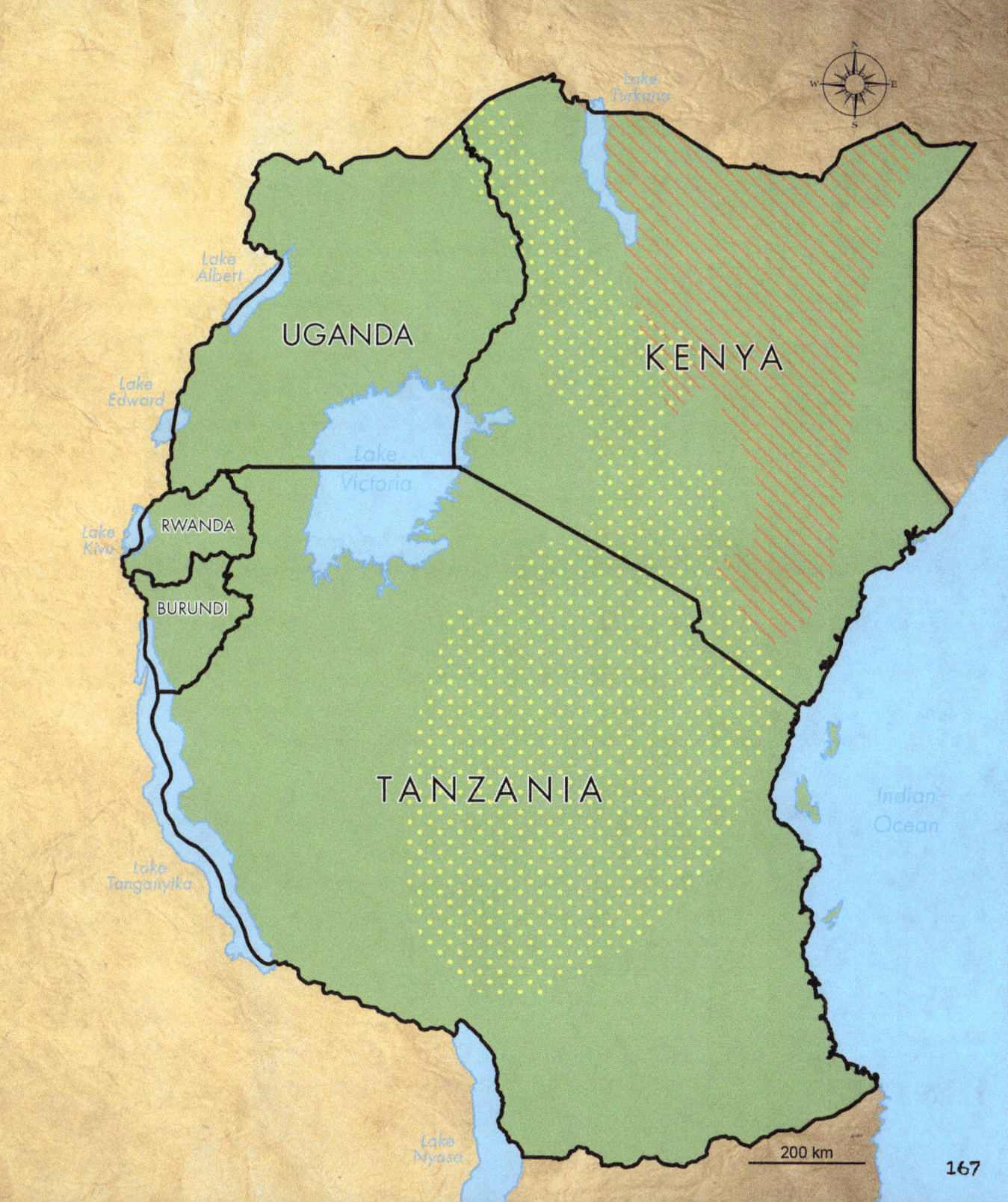

Bat
popo

You might not believe it but 20% of all mammal species in the world are bats. In East Africa alone there are over 140 different bat species. And yes, bats are mammals, not birds - they are the only mammals that are really able to fly (and not just glide from tree to tree).

Scientists have divided bats into megabats and microbats. Megabats are usually bigger and heavier than microbats but there are a few other differences. Megabats have larger eyes, claws on their wings, and most have dog or fox-like faces, smaller ears and no tails.

Megabats are also called "fruit bats", as they mainly feed on fruit, or "flying foxes", because of their fox or dog-like faces. The Pemba flying fox, that lives on Pemba Island off the Tanzanian coast, is one of the largest bats in Africa. When its wings are spread open, they are as wide as when an adult woman spreads out her arms.

Many people think that bats are blind, but this is actually not true. Megabats, for example, navigate by sight and smell. Only microbats use echolocation to find their way, but even they can see - although not as well megabats.

Echolocation works like this: The bat makes a sound and then listens to its echo to find out where objects are. Microbats are pretty good at this; they can travel in total darkness and even identify their favourite foods this way - many microbats eat insects. They trap the bugs with their wings and channel them to their mouths to feed while flying... real "fast food". ☺

Geoffroy's horseshoe bat

fruit bat

Some bats hunt and feed on bigger prey such as frogs or rodents, for example the African false vampire bat. They even eat the bones of their prey.

African straw-coloured fruit bats

large-eared free-tailed bat

Many of the bats in East Africa have fun names - since there are over 1,400 bat species in the world one has to get creative when naming them. 😊 There is for example Hildegarde's tomb bat or the Naked-rumped tomb bat. Tomb bats are often found in old tombs, that's where they got their names from.

Many bats get their names from the way they look. There are slit-faced bats, like the large-eared slit-faced bat or the dwarf slit-faced bat. They have a deep slit running from the nose to their ears. Horseshoe bats have noses that resemble horseshoes and free-tailed bats, like the African giant free-tailed bat, have long tails like mice.

flying foxes

Some bats don't have the word "bat" at all in their names, but they are still bats, for example the Banana pipistrelle, white-winged serotine, or long-haired rousette.

Egyptian slit-faced bat

🐾 Interesting fact: Vampire bats feed on the blood of mammals - but there are only three bat species that do that, and they do not live in Africa. They live in South America.

Wahlberg's fruit bat

Ostrich
mbuni

So, first of all, ostriches are birds - they can't fly, but they can run really fast. They could easily overtake the fastest human sprinter and comfortably run at that speed for miles... in fact the ostrich is the fastest animal on two legs. It is also the largest bird in the world and can weigh more than two average adult men combined.

There are two species of ostrich, the common and the Somali ostrich. They look very similar but the Somali one has blue legs. The Maasai ostrich is one of four subspecies of the common ostrich and only found in East Africa. It has a pink neck and thighs. During mating season, the Maasai ostrich male's neck and thighs become bright red.

An ostrich's first reaction to danger is to run away. Sometimes it lies down with its neck flat on the ground in the hope to be invisible to predators. But ostriches can also get pretty aggressive - they can kill a lion with one kick of their feet, which have sharp nails.

Although ostriches can't fly, they still have use for their wings. When they run, they stick them out like arms to help them keep their balance and make sharp turns. During mating season males put on flashy dance shows, waving their wings around to impress females. They also use the wings to protect their chicks from sun and rain - kind of like a "bush umbrella".

common ostrich

x 24
chicken egg
ostrich egg

Ostriches eat just about anything they come across. Plants, seeds, insects, lizards and for dessert occasionally some stones – yes, really... they help to crush the food in their stomachs.

Ostriches live in small herds (yes, a herd ☺), with a boss male, called the alpha male, and a boss female, the dominant hen. The dominant hen will only breed with the alpha male, who in turn breeds with the other hens in his harem too. When the hens are ready to lay their eggs, they all put them in the same nest, with the dominant hen's eggs best protected in the middle (each hen does still recognise her own eggs). Only the boss male and female take turns to sit on the eggs to incubate them, the hen during the day, the male at night – this is because the male's black colour camouflages him well in the dark and the female's brown during the day. After about 40 days the chicks hatch, ready to walk with their parents. Many predators feed on ostrich eggs and hunt the vulnerable chicks – only very few survive to become adults.

Ostriches have very good eyesight and can spot danger from miles away – but they are not very intelligent, especially considering their size. Their brains are smaller than their eyes, about the size of a walnut.

🐾 Interesting fact: Legend has it that ostriches bury their heads in the sand when they are scared – that is just a myth. ☺

Birds - a selection
ndege

East Africa is a bird watcher's paradise. There are hundreds of species of all kinds of sizes, colours and shapes to discover. This book would be ginormous if all of them had to be included, so here just a few birds, many of which you may come across on a safari - plus a few interesting facts.

- Male weavers weave complicated nests in tree branches; some even have entrance tunnels. Females check out the nests before choosing a male to mate.

- You can often see oxpeckers on the backs of animals, where they feed on ticks and other parasites - which the animals love. 😊

oxpecker

ground hornbill

helmeted guineafowl

shoebill

augur buzzard

ring-necked dove

lilac-breasted roller

- The shoebill is also called a whale head — you can see why. This is a huge bird, about as tall as a ten-year old child.

- Not all kingfishers eat fish and bee-eaters don't only eat bees 😊 — despite what their names say. They both like all kinds of insects.

kingfisher

secretary bird

two different species of bee-eater

silvery-cheeked hornbill

yellow-throated spurfowl

Egyptian goose

superb starling

weaver

- Hamerkop means "hammer head" in the Afrikaans language – the bird carries that name because of the hammer-like shape of its head. Hamerkops build huge nests, complete with walls, roof, entrance and a tunnel to a breeding chamber. These "mansions" are up to 50 kilogrammes heavy and 1,5 metres wide, making them the biggest bird nests in Africa.

grey-breasted spurfowl

hamerkop

- A lovebird is a species of parrot. They have this "romantic" name because lovebirds mate for life and the pairs are often found sitting together.

- Pelicans have a large throat pouch which they use to catch and scoop up fish. They then tip out the water before swallowing the fish.

- The huge marabou stork squirts pee on its legs to cool down in the African heat – that's why they look white. They often dine with the vultures on carrion.

fisheagle

marabou stork

pelican

Lovebird

waxbill

- Many people think vultures are ugly, but they are extremely important birds – and in my opinion pretty cool. They feed on carrion, even when the meat is already so rotten that other carnivores won't touch it. 😊 This way vultures prevent the spread of disease. They are the "hygiene police" of the bush.

vultures

African hoopoe

hornbill

kori bustard

- Flamingos are pink because of what they eat. When they are born, they are grey; they turn pink from the pigments in the tiny shrimps and algae they eat.

- Hornbill females seal themselves into a tree hole by closing the entrance with mud and poo before they lay their eggs. The male feeds her through a small gap and until the chicks are big enough.

heron

flamingo

- Some birds eat fruit and seeds, others feed on insects, lizards, frogs, mice or snakes. Some eat fish, carrion or grass and others eat a mix of all of those. Many birds don't need to drink water, they get the moisture from their food.

175

Some "show-off" words...

All about food

- **carnivore** — an animal that eats mostly meat
- **insectivore** — a carnivore that mainly eats insects
- **piscivore** — a carnivore that eats mainly fish
- **herbivore** — an animal that eats mostly plants
- **grazer** — a herbivore that feeds on grass and herbs
- **browser** — a herbivore that feeds on leaves, shoots and fruit from shrubs and trees
- **mixed feeder** — a herbivore that grazes and browses, feeding on all types of plants
- **frugivore** — a herbivore that eats mostly fruit
- **omnivore** — an animal that eats everything, meat and plants - humans are omnivores

tuber — thick underground stem of a plant for example a potato

- **predator** — carnivore that hunts and kills other animals to eat them
- **prey** — animals that are hunted by predators
- **scavenger** — an animal that does not hunt and kill other animals but feeds on animals that are already dead, dead plants or even rubbish
- **carrion** — rotting flesh of a dead animal
- **ruminant** — an animal that chews its food twice. Ruminants chew and swallow plants, which then go into a type of stomach called "rumen". After the food has broken down in the rumen, the animal regurgitates it (throws up into the mouth ☺); the stuff that comes up is called the "cud". Then they chew the cud again, this way they can get more nutrients out of their food
- **to ruminate** — to chew the cud (see ruminant)

Who is who in the animal kingdom?

domestic animals — pets and farm animals. They were bred over time to live with people
wild animals — wild animals are not tame, they live independent of people
vertebrate — animals with a spine / backbone. The name comes from the word "vertebrae", which is the Latin name for the spinal bones. Mammals, fish, birds, amphibians and reptiles are vertebrates — humans too
invertebrate — animals without a backbone, for example insects, worms or slugs
mammal — an animal that has glands which the female uses to feed her young with milk. Humans are mammals, too
primate — monkeys, lemurs and apes; since humans are apes, we are primates, too

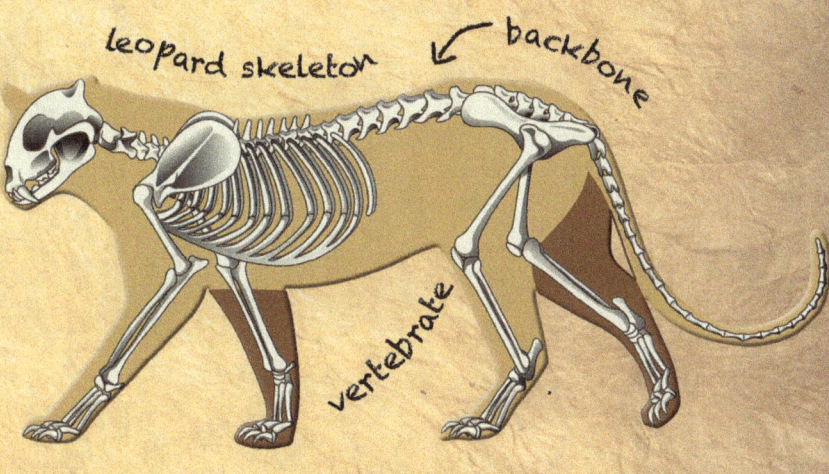
leopard skeleton — backbone — vertebrate

ungulate — an animal with hooves. There are odd-toed ungulates, like zebras or rhinos, and even-toed ungulates, like giraffe, antelopes or hippos
rodent — a mammal that has a pair of teeth both at the front of the top jaw and at the front of the bottom jaw, which keep growing throughout the animal's life. They use them to gnaw, dig and for defence. Mice and rats are rodents
cold-blooded — animals that can't control their body temperature. They need the sun to warm up and go in the shade to cool down. Snakes and crocodiles are cold-blooded, for example

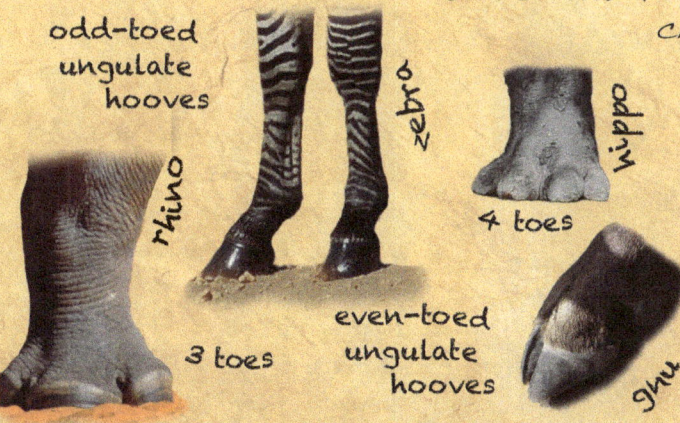
odd-toed ungulate hooves — rhino — 3 toes — zebra — hippo — 4 toes — even-toed ungulate hooves — gnu

warm-blooded — animals that can keep their body temperature higher than their environment, without needing the sun
amphibian — small vertebrates that need water, especially for breeding, such as frogs
reptile — vertebrates, such as snakes, with a skin made from bony plates or scales

Boys & girls

There are many different terms used for male, female and baby animals, depending on their species – and it is very confusing; below you'll find a few examples. If in doubt, just call them males, females and "offspring" for all the babies – then you'll never be wrong. ☺

Elephants, hippos, Antelopes etc:
females   – cow, ewe
males   – bull, ram
baby   – calf, fawn

Cats and dogs:
baby   – cub, kit, kitten, pup

male lion
lion cubs

a pride of lions
lioness

A few animals have unique names for males and females, for example "lion and lioness".

Social life of animals

Just like for "males and females", there are many different words used for groups of animals. Some examples:

herd   – group of elephants, antelopes etc.
sounder   – group of pigs
pack   – group of wild dogs
bachelor herd – group of young males
pride   – group of lions
troop   – group of baboons
harem   – group of females with a male leader

crèche   – group of young animals, which is looked after by one or a few females, while the other mothers graze or hunt; it's like a "kindergarten"

peer group   – group of young animals of similar age

Family affairs

species — species are basically different types of animals. Animals of the same species breed with each other naturally and have offspring. There are some so-called "hybrids" — babies of different species — such as "zonkeys" (a baby of a zebra and a donkey). But they are usually sterile, which means they can't produce babies themselves.

subspecies — this is a bit of a tough one to explain and not all scientists agree here all the time, but subspecies are essentially groups of animals of one species that look or behave a little different from the other groups and live in different places. For example, the Lichtenstein's hartebeest lives in western and southern Tanzania, and the Coke's hartebeest lives in central/northern Tanzania and southern Kenya — they are both subspecies of the hartebeest.

a mate — another animal of the same species to breed with. Two mates, a female and a male, make pair. Some pairs stay together for life (like dik-diks), but most animals just pair up for the time it takes to reproduce

species: waterbuck
Defassa waterbuck — subspecies
Common waterbuck — subspecies

to mate — to find a partner to reproduce. Most animals follow different mating rituals and males show off in different ways to attract the girls

mating season — the time of year where animals mate, depending on species and the natural environment

breeding — when two animals, a male and a female, reproduce, have babies ☺

on heat — when a female animal is ready to mate with a male and to become pregnant

to incubate — to keep eggs at the right temperature to develop so that the babies can hatch. For birds that means sitting on them, while turtles and crocodiles bury them

ostrich incubating eggs

baboons grooming each other

Habits

nocturnal	- active at night
crepuscular	- active at twilight (first and last light)
diurnal	- active during the day
nomadic	- animals that keep moving to find food
migratory	- animals that move to different places depending on the season
sedentary	- animals that stay in one territory and don't migrate
gregarious	- animals that live in large groups, for example monkeys
solitary	- animals that prefer to live alone, for example leopards
territorial	- animals that protect and defend a territory from other animals of the same species. Hippos are for example very territorial
dominant	- the "boss" male or female of a group; the leader
grooming	- when animals groom each other, they remove parasites or insects from each other's fur. Some antelopes do that using their teeth and primates use their hands. For apes and monkeys grooming is very important as it helps them to form bonds.

Smelly stuff

to defecate	- means "to poop"
animal latrine	- an "animal toilet", a place where some wildlife returns to poop and pee
scent glands	- some animals have glands, which produce smelly stuff, a secretion which they rub onto plants to mark their territories. These can be at different parts of their bodies, for example close to their eyes (preorbital glands) or close to their bums (anal glands)
secretion	- the stuff coming out of scent glands
scat	- poo of wild animals

dik-dik

scent gland

Body parts

front quarters	- the two front legs
hind quarters	- the two back legs
digit	- a finger or toe, for example in apes
skull	- the bone part in the head of an animal
molars	- teeth at the back of a mammal's mouth, used to grind food
incisors	- teeth in the front of most mammals' mouths, used to bite food. Hippos have the largest incisors of any land animal in their bottom jaws, they use them for fighting. Their long tusks in the top jaw are canine teeth
canines	- teeth mostly used to tear food, carnivores and many other animals have them
tusks	- they are either really long incisors, like in elephants, or long canine teeth, like in the hippo's top jaw
horns	- they are made of keratin, just like fingernails. Unlike deer, that lose their antlers once a year, antelopes don't shed their horns. Horns also never have branches like antlers

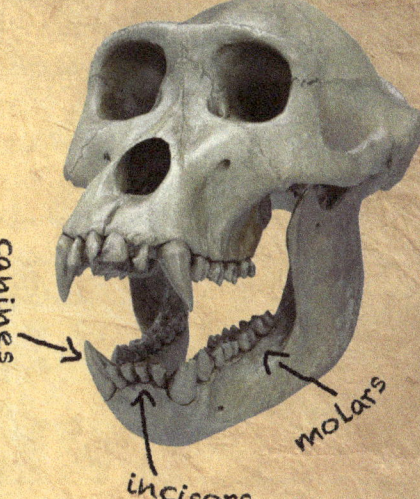
gorilla skull

Where is home...?

ecosystem — an area where living things, such as animals and plants, together with non-living elements, like temperature and water, create a special environment. Examples: savanna, rain forest, desert...

habitat — a place where an animal or a plant lives and finds everything they need to survive, for example mates, food, water and shelter

dry / wet season — in East Africa, there are no seasons like cold winters and warm summers. The year is divided into two dry seasons and two wet seasons. In the dry seasons it rains very little or not at all and many waterholes and streams dry up. During the wet seasons it rains a lot. All life here is adjusted to dry and wet periods

January — dry — April — wet — July — dry — December — wet

native species — a species that lives in the area where it naturally developed

Alien / non-native species — were brought into an area by people at some point

endemic species — a species that naturally occurs only in a certain area and nowhere else. For example, the Ader's duiker is endemic to Zanzibar Island

brackish water — a mix of freshwater and seawater, often found where rivers flow into the sea

savanna — an ecosystem with a mix of woodland and grassland

aquatic — animals that live in water most of the time, for example sea turtles

semi-aquatic — animals that spend similar amounts of time in the water as on land, for example hippos

terrestrial — animals that live on land, for example lions

camouflaged — when an animal blends in well with its surroundings / is well hidden

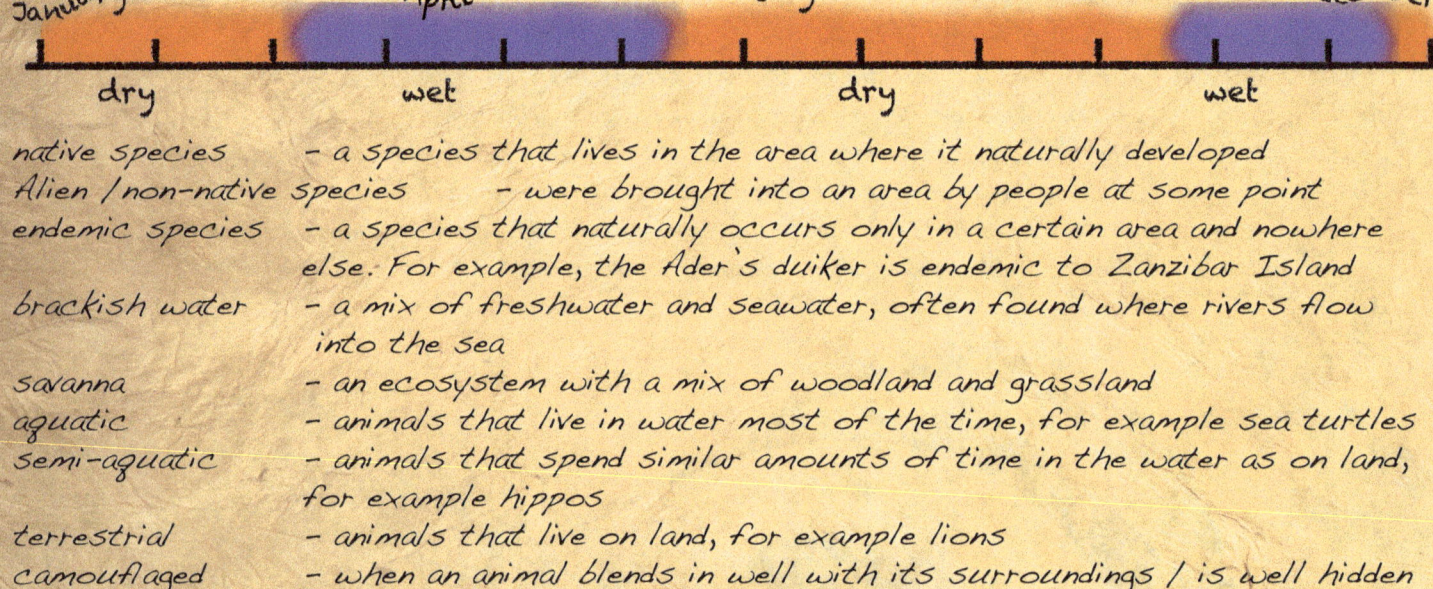

savanna - inside the Ngorongoro Crater in Tanzania

A bit of science...

symbiosis — when two different species interact and benefit each other. For example the oxpecker picking parasites off the buffalo's back - the oxpecker benefits by getting food, the buffalo is freed from annoying insects

parasite — they live in or on animals and feed from those animals - for example ticks, lice and tapeworms that feed off their hosts' blood

DNA — contains all information about how a living being looks and functions; it is in all cells - even a human's. DNA is inherited from generation to generation and responsible for all individuals of one species looking similar

camouflage
spot the leopard... ☺

buffalo in symbiosis with an oxpecker

Languages

Afrikaans — language originating from European languages spoken in southern Africa, especially South Africa and Namibia

Swahili — most people in East Africa speak Swahili, also called Kiswahili and it is an official language in Tanzania, Kenya, Uganda and Rwanda

Somali — language spoken in north-eastern Kenya and Somalia

Luganda — language native to Uganda

Kirundi — an official language in Burundi, but also spoken in other countries

Credits

Cover: all photos - Wayne Hendry, map - Birgit Hendry
All drawings & illustrations: Wayne & Birgit Hendry
Backgrounds: ikostudio / stock.adobe.com; Aelita / stock.adobe.com; robynmac / stock.adobe.com; Lumos sp / stock.adobe.com; Lotus _studio / shutterstock.com
Acknowledgements: photo - Wayne Hendry
Foreword: all photos - African People & Wildlife
Introduction and A few lessons from Africa: Wayne & Birgit Hendry
East Africa: Kilimanjaro - Lubo Invanko / shutterstock.com; World map - Tartila / thehungryjpeg.com; East Africa map: Mark Shand; turaco - Serguei Koultchitskii/ shutterstock.com; gorilla - Attila JANDI / shutterstock.com; lion - RujStudio / shutterstock.com
The big Icons - Map: giraffe & buffalo - Wayne Hendry; elephant - Patryk Kosmider / Shutterstock.com; rhino - Martha van Tonder / shutterstock.com
Cape buffalo: left - MartinMaritz / Shutterstock.com; bottom panorama - Roger de la Harpe / Shutterstock; skull & muddy buffalo - Wayne Hendry; oxpeckers - Michael Potter 11 / Shutterstock.com
African Elephant: bottom with Kilimanjaro - Paul Hampton / Shutterstock.com; cow with calf: Kletr / Shutterstock.com; elephant dung - Anke van Wyk / Shutterstock.com; mock charge - javarman / stock.adobe.com
Giraffe: giraffe drinking - Nicola_K_photos / Shutterstock; giraffe head bottom left – Laura Gomez / stock.adobe.com; all other photos - Wayne Hendry
Rhinoceros: panorama photo bottom - Yakov Oskanov / Shutterstock.com; rhino profile left - claudia Otte / stock.adobe.com; top right – Wayne Hendry, bottom right - Birgit Hendry

Some spiral horns - Map: Eland, Sitatunga, Bongo, Greater & Lesser kudu - Wayne Hendry; Bushbuck - PeterBetts / fotolia.com
Eland Antelope: profile bottom left - Greens and Blues / Shutterstock.com; all other photos - Wayne Hendry
Greater kudu: male adult bottom left – Nadine Haase / stock.adobe.com; young kudu bull – EcoView / stock.adobe.com; bull top right – PeterBetts / Fotolia.com; female bottom right – Spargel / stock.adobe.com
Lesser kudu: top middle – Impala / stock.adobe.com; female bottom middle – Martina Berg / adobe.stock.com; all others – Wayne Hendry
Sitatunga: female left – Any Art Netty / Shutterstock.com; landscape left – Wayne Hendry; young bull, right – Jiri Cvrk / shutterstock.com; bull lying down – aldaer / stock.adobe.com, sitatunga bull top right – Robert Rusch / shutterstock.com; sitatunga calf – Eric Isselée / shutterstock.com
East African Bushbuck: male bushbuck bottom left & male bushbuck second from right - PeterBetts / fotolia.com; baby bushbuck bottom – Dafna Ben nun / shutterstock.com; bushbuck in forest – Wayne Hendry; bushbuck female top right – Renate Wefers / stock.adobe.com
Eastern bongo: bongo middle left page - poeticpenguin / Shutterstock.com; bongo bottom left – Ryan M. Bolton / Shutterstock.com; bongo top right – René Warburg; bongo right page bottom – Keitma / Shutterstock.com; bongo calf – Pascale Gueret / shutterstock.com; Aberdares landscape – Rich Carey / shutterstock.com

Large antelopes and zebra - Map: Waterbuck, wildebeest, sable, roan, zebra – Wayne Hendry
Waterbuck: Defassa waterbuck male, female and youngster – Wayne Hendry; Waterbuck male top right – Birgit Hendry; female and calf – Moehring / shutterstock.com
Sable Antelope: Bulls fighting – wyssu / stock.adobe.com; herd bottom left and bull with cows bottom right – Wayne Hendry; male bottom right – Any-Kim Möller / stock.adobe.com; yearling top middle – jindrich_pavelka / shutterstock.com
Roan antelope: Roan middle left – Wayne Hendry; roan lying down bottom left – Ruth Hallam / stock.adobe.com; group of roan top right – EcoView / stock.adobe.com; roan bottom right – Wayne Hendry
Zebra: Grevy zebra – Christian Musat / shutterstock.com; single zebra top middle – Eric Isseléee / stock.adobe.com; zebra sunset, zebra pair top right, zebras drinking and zebra skull – Wayne Hendry
Wildebeest: Running Nyasa wildebeest bottom left - Mark Sheridan-Johnson / shutterstock.com; two photos middle – Wayne Hendry; migration right – Dennis Stogsdill / shutterstock.com

Medium antelopes - Map: Impala, topi, hartebeest - Wayne Hendry; reedbuck - Maggy Meyer / shuttertsock.com, puku – Sharon Haeger / shutterstock.com, kob – Jukka Jantunen / shutterstock.com
Impala: females left, young rams fighting bottom right and two males bottom right – Wayne Hendry; impala running top right – sitayi / shutterstock.com; male impala middle right – outdoorsman / stock.adobe.com
Topi: topi with calf – Eric Isseléee / stock.adobe.com; topi left - RMFerreira / shutterstock.com; all others – Wayne Hendry

Puku: group bottom left and puku fighting – Jez Bennett / shutterstock.com; puku herd right – sitayi / shutterstock.com; puku mother and calf – Federica Cordero / shutterstock.com; male puku right – Sharon Haeger / shutterstock.com
Hartebeest: Lelwel left - Oleg Znamenskiy / shutterstock.com; hirola – OliverZeid / shutterstock.com; all on right – Wayne Hendry
Reedbuck: common male left – michael luckett / adobe.stock.com; bottom left common females - paco como / shutterstock.com; top bohor female – slowmotiongli / shutterstock.com; bohor males top right - Cezary Wojtkowski / shutterstock.com; mountain reedbuck female bottom middle – Duncan Noakes / stock.adobe.com; mountain male right – Jonathan Pledger / shutterstock.com
Kob: bottom left and females bottom right - Oleg Znamenskiy / shutterstock.com; running kob and fighting kob top right - Jukka Jantunen / shutterstock.com; top right two running kob – Martin Mecnarowski / shutterstock.com

Small antelopes - Map: Dik-dik - BlueOrange Studio / adobe.stock.com; Klipspringer – Birgit Hendry; Sharpe's Grysbok - Paco Como / shutterstock.com; Duiker - Four Oaks / shutterstock.com; Steenbok – Michael Potter 11 / shutterstock.com; Oribi – Jaco van Rensburg / shutterstock.com; Suni - Olexandr Taranukhin / shutterstock.com;
Dik-dik: "hairstyle" portrait bottom – Eric Isselée / adobe.stock.com; dik-dik bottom right – BlueOrange Studio / adobe.stock.com; dik-dik bottom left, top right and middle – Wayne Hendry
Duiker: Bush duiker bottom left – Chris Fourie / stock.adobe.com; red duiker – feathercollector / shutterstock.com; bush duiker top middle – Alta Oosthuizen / adobe.stock.com; Ader's duiker – Wayne Hendry; blue duiker – Four Oaks / shutterstock.com; yellow-backed duiker – K Hanley CHDPhoto / shutterstock.com
Steenbok: male left – Nicholas James 101 / shutterstock.com; female bottom – Gert Frey / adobe.stock.com; male middle – EcoView / adobe.stock.com; top right – Michael Potter 11 / shutterstock.com; female bottom right – Mytho / adobe.stock.com
Klipspringer: top middle, bottom right, middle left, landscape – Wayne Hendry; female head – sitayi / shutterstock.com; top right – Richard Seeley / shutterstock.com, feet – https://commons.wikimedia.org/wiki/User:MONGO
Oribi: bottom left and top right – Wayne Hendry; top middle – Black Sheep media / shutterstock.com; oribi baby – Tarpan / shutterstock.com; bottom right – Jaco van Rensburg / shutterstock.com
Suni: top left and bottom right – VladKK / shutterstock.com; bottom left and middle right – Olexandr Taranukhin / shutterstock.com;
Grysbok: portrait left and bottom – Paco Como / shutterstock.com; right – Peter Mullineux / shutterstock.com

Cats & cat-likes - Map: Lion – RujStudio / shutterstock.com; Cheetah - Frank Wiechens / stock.adobe.com; African Golden Cat - flpa-images.co.uk; Caracal – Stu Porter / shutterstock.com; Leopard – BearFotos / shutterstock.com; Serval – Christoph Hähnel / adobe.stock.com; Genet - A.S.Floro / shutterstock.com; Civet – AndreAnita – shutterstock.com; African Wildcat – Johan Barnard / shutterstock.com
Lion: Lioness with cub – Johann Mader / shutterstock.com; male and female bottom left and lion in tree – Wayne Hendry; male top middle – EcoView / stock.adobe.com; two cubs – Theodore Mattas / shutterstock.com; profile right – Melissa Schalke / stock.adobe.com; paw print in sand – Villiers Steyn / shutterstock.com
Leopard: Leopard left – Wayne Hendry; leopard in tree top right – fotolia.com; leopard in tree right – satishyewlekar / shutterstock.com; female with cub – Stu Porter / shutterstock.com
Cheetah: cheetah bottom left – Wayne Hendry; cheetah mother with cubs – Othman Al-Bedaiwi; cheetah top right – Frank Wiechens / stock.adobe.com; running cheetahs – photobar /shutterstock.com; cheetah on rock – Eric Isselée / shutterstock.com
Serval: middle right - Christoph Hähnel / adobe.stock.com; left – Morten Ross / shutterstock.com; bottom left – Samib123 / shutterstock.com; bottom right – Roger de la Harpe / shutterstock.com
Caracal: mother with kitten and kitten – Ondrej Chvatal / shutterstock.com; caracal on tree – Stu Porter / shutterstock.com; bottom right – Andrej Prosicky / shutterstock.com
Genet: left in tree – A.S.Floro / shutterstock.com; right middle – Villiers Steyn / shutterstock.com; bottom right – reptiles4all / shutterstock.com
Civet: young civets right – Mark Sheridan-Johnson / shutterstock.com; bottom right – Martin Mecnarowski / shutterstock.com; bottom left – Francesco de marco / shutterstock.com
African Wildcat: Left – Maggy Meyer / shutterstock.com; bottom left – EcoPrint / shutterstock.com; face – John Queenan / shutterstock.com; under tree – EcoPrint / shutterstock.com; middle – Ondrej Prosicky / shutterstock.com; kittens – Erwin Niemand / shutterstock.com
African Golden Cat: flpa-images.co.uk

Other predators - Map: spotted hyena – EcoView / stock.adobe.com; striped hyena - Eric Isselée / stock.adobe.com; aardwolf - Cathy Withers-Clarke / shutterstock.com; honey badger - Vladimir Wrangel / shutterstock.com; Golden Wolf - Scott Ward / shutterstock.com; bat-eared fox - Daniel Zuppinger / shutterstock.com; side-striped jackal – Chris Fourie / shutterstock.com; Black-backed jackal – Wim Hoek / shutterstock.com; wild dog – GoodFocused / shutterstock.com

Hyena: Striped hyena left – Eric Isselée /stock.adobe.com; hyena with cub – Stu Porter / shutterstock.com; aardwolf middle – Cathy Withers-Clarke / shutterstock.com; hyena with black cub – Maggy Meyer / shutterstock.com; aardwolf bottom right – Joe McDonald / shutterstock.com; top middle and bottom middle – Wayne Hendry

African wild dog: middle left – fotografie4you / shutterstock.com; young dog – imageBroker.com / shutterstock.com; three dogs - J Reineke / shutterstock.com; group under tree right – Jez Bennett / shutterstock.com; pack bottom right – Ewan Chesser / shutterstock.com; bottom right – Thomas Retterath shutterstock.com

Bat-eared fox: landscape bottom left – Wijnand vT / shutterstock.com; top middle – Robert Hardholt / stock.adobe.com; bottom middle – Daniel Zuppinger / shutterstock.com; kit and mother – Danita Delimont / shutterstock.com; top right lying down – Paul Tessier / shutterstock.com; bottom left and bottom right – Wayne Hendry; termite – Pan Xunbin / shutterstock.com

Jackal: bottom left – Eric Isselée / shutterstock.com; pup – Albie Venter / shuttertsock.com, three pups at den – Dmussman / shutterstock.com; side-striped jackal right – Chris Fourie / shutterstock.com; howling jackal – Chris Fourie / stock.adobe.com; top right and bottom – Wayne Hendry / shutterstock.com

African Golden Wolf: right – Scott Ward / shutterstock.com; left – Wayne Hendry

Honey Badger: left - Vladimir Wrangel / shutterstock.com; middle and top right – Paco Como / shutterstock.com; bottom left – Braam Collins / shutterstock.com; bottom right – Vladimir Wrangel / shutterstock.com

Maasailand - Map: Oryx, Thomson's gazelle, Grant's gazelle – Wayne Hendry, Gerenuk - nwdph / shutterstock.com; Robert's gazelle – lexan / adobe.stock.com

Gerenuk: female left – Charles Aghoian / stock.adobe.com; male middle bottom – PixilRay / stock.adobe.com, gerenuk feeding middle – impala / stock.adobe.com; mother and fawn – MicheleB / shutterstock.com; gerenuk right – sitayi / shutterstock.com; top middle – kyslynskahal / shutterstock.com

Thomson's Gazelle: ram left, bottom middle left and middle right – Wayne Hendry; top middle – Deborah Benbrook / stock.adobe.com; mother with fawn – paula french – shutterstock.com; herd bottom right – Sebastien Burel / fotolia.com

Oryx: bottom left and bottom right – Axel Gutjahr / stock.adobe.com; top right and bottom middle – Wayne Hendry

Grant's Gazelle: middle left and Robert's gazelle – Wayne Hendry; top middle – Karlos Lomsky – stock.adobe.com; herd bottom left – Oleg Znamenskiy / shutterstock.com; bottom right – impala / stock.adobe.com

In the water - Map: Otter – Don Fink / shutterstock.com; crocodile and hippos – Wayne Hendry

Hippo: bottom left and bottom middle – Wayne Hendry; fighting bulls – Anton_Ivanov / shutterstock.com; mother with baby – Henk Bogaard; bottom right – Anan Kaewkhammul / shutterstock.com

Crocodile: middle left – James Arup / shutterstock.com; middle bottom – cris13 / stock.adobe.com; baby hatching – Jonathan Oberholster / stock.adobe.com; top right, bottom right – Wayne Hendry; bottom left – Stu Porter / shutterstock.com

Otter: bottom left – John Peter Davies / shutterstock.com; middle left, clawless otter top, two otters bottom – Max Allen / shutterstock.com; right – Nagel Photography / shutterstock.com

Apes & Monkey - Map: Vervet monkey – Eric Isselée / stock.adobe.com; Gorilla – Attila Jandi – shutterstock.com; Chimpanzee – Cristi Popescu / shutterstock.com; Syke's monkey – Impala / shuttertsock.com; black & white colobus – red-feniks / shutterstock.com; baboon – NaturesMomentsuk / shutterstock.com

Vervet monkey: top middle – Wayne Hendry; bottom left – Stephen Lew / shutterstock.com; top right – Gerrit de Vries / stock.adobe.com; bottom middle – David_Steele / stock.adobe.com; bottom right - Eric Isselée / stock.adobe.com

Baboon: yellow baboons – Alexandra Giese / shutterstock.com; all others – Wayne Hendry

A few more monkeys: Zanzibar red colobus – Ryan M. Bolton / shutterstock.com; Syke's monkey – Impala / stock.adobe.com; colobus middle – red-feniks / shuttertsock.com; blue monkey, red-tailed monkey and red colobus – Wayne Hendry; colobus with baby – Vaclav Matous / shutterstock.com

Chimpanzee: all – Wayne Hendry

Gorilla: male left – dptro / shutterstock.com; gorilla with baby top middle – Gudkov Andrey / shutterstock.com; silverback - Brina L. Bunt / shutterstock.com; young gorilla top right – Lmspencer – shutterstock.com; gorilla group – Mary Ann McDonald / shutterstock.com; bottom right hand – Axel Kohler / shutterstock.com

What to spot at night - Map: Zorilla, aardvark, porcupine and hedgehog - Eric Isselée / shutterstock.com; pangolin – Kobie Douglas / shutterstock.com; bushbaby – Rosa Jay / shutterstock.com; African striped weasel - flpa-images.co.uk
Aardvark: top left – Paul Wishart / shutterstock.com; running left – Stacey Ann Alberts; bottom – Kelsey Green / shutterstock.com
Pangolin: top right – 2630ben / shutterstock.com; curled up and scales – Eugene Troskie / shutterstock.com; bottom right – Hein Myers Photography / shutterstock.com; bottom middle - Kobie Douglas / shutterstock.com
Hedgehog: with baby – Eric Isselée / shutterstock.com; left – Kuttelvaserova Stuchelova / shutterstock.com; right – Best dog photo / shutterstock.com
Porcupine: top right – bayazed / shutterstock.com; cape porcupine – Stacey Ann Alberts / shutterstock.com; brush-tailed porcupine – teekayu / shutterstock.com; bottom left – EcoPrint / shutterstock.com; quills – Anke van Wyk / shutterstock.com; bottom right - Eric Isselée / stock.adobe.com
Zorilla & Striped weasel: both images - flpa-images.co.uk
Bushbaby & Galago: Thick-tailed galago – shutterstock.com; Senegal bushbaby – Vladislav T. Jirousek; greater galago – Mark Sheridan-Johnson / shutterstock.com; lesser bushbaby – Alta Oosthuizen / shutterstock.com

Pigs - Map: Bushpig – Villiers Steyn / shutterstock.com; warthog – Wayne Hendry; red river hog – Eric Isselée / shutterstock.com; giant forest hog – huang jenhung / shutterstock.com
Bushpig: all – Stu Porter / shutterstock.com
Warthog: hog in hole – clickit / shutterstock.com; warthog with piglets – Rudi Hulshof / shutterstock.com; piglets kneeling – Andrzej Kubik / shutterstock.com; warthog drinking – Ant Haynes / shutterstock.com; warthogs running away – Alta Oosthuizen / shutterstock.com
Giant Forest Hog: huang jenhung / shutterstock.com
Red River Hog: group left - J. Natayo / shutterstock.com; bottom right - Eric Isselée / shutterstock.com

Other little guys - Map: Tree Hyrax - tony mills / shutterstock.com; Rock Hyrax – Jeffrey B. Banke / shutterstock.com; rat – Rosa Jay / shutterstock.com; Mongoose – Krakenimages.com; Squirrel -Paco Como / adobe.stock.com; Hare – Joe McDonald / shutterstock.com
Hyrax: tree hyrax – tony mills / shutterstock.com; rock hyraxes – Magdanatka / shutterstock.com; group bottom – Photocreo Michal Bednarek / shutterstock.com; top right – Volker Haag / shutterstock.com
Mongoose: Dwarf mongoose – Jen Watson / shutterstock.com; slender mongoose – Paco Como / shutterstock.com; white-tailed mongoose – Iwan Kuzmin / shutterstock.com; dwarf mongoose middle right – Binson Calfort / shutterstock.com; mongoose in background – Stacey Ann Alberts / shutterstock.com; banded mongoose – David Malec / shutterstock.com; mongoose bottom right – Wayne Hendry
Mole, shrew, gerbil, mouse & rat: golden-rumped elephant shrew and elephant shrew top – Marius Dobilas / shutterstock.com; acacia tree rat – EcoPrint / shutterstock.com; pygmy door mouse – Punyaphat Larpsomboon / shutterstock.com; four-striped grass rat – Karer Bartik / shutterstock.com; naked mole-rat – Eric Isselée; top right and middle – Wayne Hendry / shutterstock.com; bottom right – MattiATH / shutterstock.com
Squirrel: left – Cathy Withers-Clarke / shutterstock.com; right – Stefano Cavanna
Hare & Rabbit: Ear – John Michael Vosloo / shutterstock.com; African savannah hare – NaturesMomentsuk / shutterstock.com; Cape hare – Stritchy / shutterstock.com; bottom right – Bartosz Budrewicz / shutterstock.com

Some scaly creatures - Map: tortoise – Jeffrey B. Banke / shutterstock.com; snake – Paul Vinten / shutterstock.com; terrapin – EcoView / adobe.stock.com; sea turtle – Simon Eeman / shutterstock.com; lizard – Delbards / shutterstock.com; sea snake – NickEvansKZN / shutterstock.com; chameleon – imadldk / shutterstock.com
Lizard & Chameleon: East Usambara Pygmy chameleon and Taita blade-horned chameleon – Ferdy Timmerman / shutterstock.com; Rainbow Jackson's chameleon – scott hughey / shutterstock.com; agama – Wayne Hendry; both green keel-bellied lizardss and Usambara giant three-horned chameleon – reptiles4all / shutterstock.com; baby yellow-crested Jackson's chameleon – Jason Mintzer / shutterstock.com; Fischer's chameleon – Milan Zygmunt / shutterstock.com; monitor lizard – Arnoud Quanjer / shutterstock.com; Helmeted chameleon – Nick Henn / shutterstock.com; gecko – Photozi / adobe.stock.com; African striped skink – Shona / adobe.stock.com
Tortoise, terrapin & turtle: green turtle left and baby turtle right – Magdalena Paluchowska / shutterstock.com; tortoise bottom left – Wayne Hendry; terrapin on hippo – EcoView - stock.adobe.com; loggerhead turtles – Anita Martingano; tortoise head – Pajac Slovensky / shutterstock.com; leopard tortoise – Po S Chan; baby turtles bottom middle – Simon Eeman and green sea turtle / shutterstock.com
Snake: puffadder – Peter Mullineux / shutterstock.com; green mamba left and black mamba – reptiles4all / shutterstock.com; sea snake and spitting cobra bottom middle – NickEvansKZN / shutterstock.com; African rock python – Albie Venter / shutterstock.com; green mamba right – nra / shutterstock.com; spitting cobra right – Stu Porter / shutterstock.com

Wings & Feathers - Map: Common ostrich – Andrzej Kubik / shutterstock.com; Somali ostrich – Steve Tum / shutterstock.com, bat – Rosa Jay / shutterstock.com, lovebirds – H. van der Winden

Bats: bat face left – shutterstock.com; bottom middle left – Jukka Jantunen / shutterstock.com; top middle and top right – Ivan Kuzmin / shutterstock.com; flying foxes and background right – Tetyana Dotsenko / shutterstock.com; bottom middle left – aaltair / shutterstock.com; bottom right – Uwe Bergwitz / shutterstock.com

Ostrich: left with chicks – Dmussman – shutterstock.com; herd at bottom – Travel Stock / shutterstock.com; chicks top middle – Eric Isselée / shutterstock.com; top right – Alexander Barmak / shutterstock.com; Somali ostrich – Steve Tum / shutterstock.com; pair with chicks – sirtravelalot / shutterstock.com; bottom right – Andrzej Kubik / shutterstock.com; eggs – Baishev / shutterstock.com

A few birds - Page 1: oxpecker – shutterstock.com; ground hornbill – ground hornbill – nwdph / shutterstock.com; helmeted guinea fowl – Wayne Hendry; shoebill – Silvia Truessel / shutterstock.com; augur buzzard – Marius Dobilas – shutterstock.com; ring-necked dove – Mike Dexter / shutterstock.com; lilac-breasted roller in flight – Johan Swanepoel / shutterstock.com; lilac-breasted roller on branch – Lasse Johannsson / shutterstock.com; secretary bird – Michael Potter11 / shutterstock.com; carmine bee-eater top right – DirkR / adobe.stock.com; white-fronted bee-eater in flight – Wirestock Creators / shutterstock.com; kingfisher – Ondrej Prosicky / shutterstock.com; yellow-throated spurfowl and Egyptian goose – Wayne Hendry; silvery-cheeked hornbill and weaver – Marius Dobilas / shutterstock.com; superb starlings – Sergey Uryadnikov / shutterstock.com

Page 2: grey-breasted spurfowl – Paul Tessier / shutterstock.com; hamerkop – Arthur Freixo Seixas; fisheagle – Roger de la Harpe / shutterstock.com; marabou stork, waxbill, pelican, kori bustard and heron – Wayne Hendry; lovebirds – Thomas Retterath / shutterstock.com; vultures – Rudi Hulshof / shutterstock.com; hoopoe – Thomas Retterath / shutterstock.com; hornbill – Victor Lapaev / shutterstock.com; flamingo – James Steidl / adobe.stock.com

A couple of show-off words - Page 1: leopard skeleton – BlueRingMedia / shutterstock.com; animal feet and potato – Wayne Hendry
Page 2: male lion – RujStudio / shutterstock.com; cubs – Theodore Mattas / shutterstock.com; lions on rock – Henk Bogaard / shutterstock.com; Defassa waterbuck – Wayne Hendry; common waterbuck – Birgit Hendry; ostrich – Dominique de La Croix / shutterstuck.com
Page 3: baboons, dikdik, elephant, sable and chimp foot – Wayne Hendry; hippo – Rolf Langohr; skull – ivanpavlisko / shutterstock.com
Page 4: crater – SHch / shutterstock.com; leopard in tree – Wayne Hendry; buffalo – 2630ben / shutterstock.com

The species distributions maps have been created by the author, with the support of Mike Shand, using a topographic base map and Adobe Illustrator data by him, and GIS data with the permission of the IUCN:

African elephant. IUCN SSC African Elephant Specialist Group 2021. *Loxodonta africana*. The IUCN Red List of Threatened Species. Version 2022-2. https://www.iucnredlist.org. Downloaded on 23.1.2023.
Cape buffalo. IUCN (International Union for Conservation of Nature) 2008. *Syncerus caffer*. The IUCN Red List of Threatened Species. Version 2022-2. https://www.iucnredlist.org. Downloaded on 23.1.2023.
Giraffe. IUCN (International Union for Conservation of Nature) 2018. *Giraffa camelopardalis*. The IUCN Red List of Threatened Species. Version 2022-2. https://www.iucnredlist.org. Downloaded on 23.1.2023.
Rhinoceros. *Diceros bicornis*. numerous sources / interviews.
Eland. IUCN (International Union for Conservation of Nature) 2008. *Tragelaphus oryx*. The IUCN Red List of Threatened Species. Version 2022-2. https://www.iucnredlist.org. Downloaded on 26.1.2023.
Sitatunga. IUCN (International Union for Conservation of Nature) 2008. *Tragelaphus spekii*. The IUCN Red List of Threatened Species. Version 2022-2. https://www.iucnredlist.org. Downloaded on 26.1.2023.
Bongo. IUCN (International Union for Conservation of Nature) 2008. *Tragelaphus eurycerus*. The IUCN Red List of Threatened Species. Version 2022-2. https://www.iucnredlist.org. Downloaded on 26.1.2023.
Greater kudu. IUCN (International Union for Conservation of Nature) 2016. *Tragelaphus strepsiceros*. The IUCN Red List of Threatened Species. Version 2022-2. https://www.iucnredlist.org. Downloaded on 30.1.2023.
Bushbuck. IUCN (International Union for Conservation of Nature) 2008. *Tragelaphus scriptus*. The IUCN Red List of Threatened Species. Version 2022-2. https://www.iucnredlist.org. Downloaded on 30.1.2023.
Waterbuck. IUCN (International Union for Conservation of Nature) 2008. *Kobus ellipsiprymnus*. The IUCN Red List of Threatened Species. Version 2022-2. https://www.iucnredlist.org. Downloaded on 19.1.2023.
Common wildebeest. IUCN (International Union for Conservation of Nature) 2016. *Connochaetes taurinus*. The IUCN Red List of Threatened Species. Version 2022-2. https://www.iucnredlist.org. Downloaded on 19.1.2023.
Sable antelope. IUCN (International Union for Conservation of Nature) 2008. *Hippotragus niger*. The IUCN Red List of Threatened Species. Version 2022-2. https://www.iucnredlist.org. Downloaded on 3.1.2023.

Roan antelope. IUCN (International Union for Conservation of Nature) 2008. *Hippotragus equinus*. The IUCN Red List of Threatened Species. Version 2022-2. https://www.iucnredlist.org. Downloaded on 3.1.2023.
Plains zebra. IUCN (International Union for Conservation of Nature) 2016. *Equus quagga*. The IUCN Red List of Threatened Species. Version 2022-2. https://www.iucnredlist.org. Downloaded on 3.1.2023.
Grevy zebra. IUCN (International Union for Conservation of Nature) 2016. *Equus grevyi*. The IUCN Red List of Threatened Species. Version 2022-2. https://www.iucnredlist.org. Downloaded on 3.1.2023.
Impala. IUCN (International Union for Conservation of Nature) 2016. *Aepyceros melampus*. The IUCN Red List of Threatened Species. Version 2022-2. https://www.iucnredlist.org. Downloaded on 30.1.2023.
Topi. IUCN (International Union for Conservation of Nature) 2016. *Damaliscus lunatus*. The IUCN Red List of Threatened Species. Version 2022-2. https://www.iucnredlist.org. Downloaded on 30.1.2023.
Hartebeest. IUCN (International Union for Conservation of Nature) 2016. *Alcelaphus buselaphus*. The IUCN Red List of Threatened Species. Version 2022-2. https://www.iucnredlist.org. Downloaded on 30.1.2023.
Hirola. IUCN (International Union for Conservation of Nature) 2008. *Beatragus hunteri*. The IUCN Red List of Threatened Species. Version 2022-2. https://www.iucnredlist.org. Downloaded on 30.1.2023.
Bohor reedbuck. IUCN (International Union for Conservation of Nature) 2008. *Redunca redunca*. The IUCN Red List of Threatened Species. Version 2022-2. https://www.iucnredlist.org. Downloaded on 30.1.2023.
Common reedbuck. IUCN (International Union for Conservation of Nature) 2016. *Redunca arundinum*. The IUCN Red List of Threatened Species. Version 2022-2. https://www.iucnredlist.org. Downloaded on 3.2.3023.
Mountain reedbuck. IUCN (International Union for Conservation of Nature) 2008. *Redunca fulvorufula*. The IUCN Red List of Threatened Species. Version 2022-2. https://www.iucnredlist.org. Downloaded on 3.2.3023.
Puku. IUCN (International Union for Conservation of Nature) 2016. *Kobus vardonii*. The IUCN Red List of Threatened Species. Version 2022-2. https://www.iucnredlist.org. Downloaded on 3.2.3023.
Kob. IUCN (International Union for Conservation of Nature) 2008. *Kobus kob*. The IUCN Red List of Threatened Species. Version 2022-2. https://www.iucnredlist.org. Downloaded on 3.2.3023.
Kirk's dik-dik. IUCN (International Union for Conservation of Nature) 2008. *Madoqua kirkii*. The IUCN Red List of Threatened Species. Version 2022-2. https://www.iucnredlist.org. Downloaded on 8.2.2023.
Guenther's dik-dik. IUCN (International Union for Conservation of Nature) 2016. *Madoqua guentheri*. The IUCN Red List of Threatened Species. Version 2022-2. https://www.iucnredlist.org. Downloaded on 8.2.2023.
Klipspringer. IUCN (International Union for Conservation of Nature) 2016. *Oreotragus oreotragus*. The IUCN Red List of Threatened Species. Version 2022-2. https://www.iucnredlist.org. Downloaded on 8.2.2023.
Sharpe's grysbok. IUCN (International Union for Conservation of Nature) 2008. *Raphicerus sharpei*. The IUCN Red List of Threatened Species. Version 2022-2. https://www.iucnredlist.org. Downloaded on 8.2.2023.
Steenbok. IUCN (International Union for Conservation of Nature) 2008. *Raphicerus campestris*. The IUCN Red List of Threatened Species. Version 2022-2. https://www.iucnredlist.org. Downloaded on 8.2.2023.
Common duiker. IUCN (International Union for Conservation of Nature) 2008. *Sylvicapra grimmia*. The IUCN Red List of Threatened Species. Version 2022-2. https://www.iucnredlist.org. Downloaded on 8.2.2023.
Blue duiker. IUCN (International Union for Conservation of Nature) 2016. *Philantomba monticola*. The IUCN Red List of Threatened Species. Version 2022-2. https://www.iucnredlist.org. Downloaded on 8.2.2023.
Ader's duiker. IUCN (International Union for Conservation of Nature) 2017. *Cephalophus adersi*. The IUCN Red List of Threatened Species. Version 2022-2. https://www.iucnredlist.org. Downloaded on 8.2.2023.
Oribi. IUCN (International Union for Conservation of Nature) 2016. *Ourebia ourebi*. The IUCN Red List of Threatened Species. Version 2022-2. https://www.iucnredlist.org. Downloaded on 8.2.2023.
Suni. IUCN (International Union for Conservation of Nature) 2016. *Nesotragus moschatus*. The IUCN Red List of Threatened Species. Version 2022-2. https://www.iucnredlist.org. Downloaded on 8.2.2023.
Lion. Panthera and WCS 2016. *Panthera leo*. The IUCN Red List of Threatened Species. Version 2022-2. https://www.iucnredlist.org. Downloaded on 13.2.2023.
Cheetah. IUCN SSC Cat Specialist Group 2022. *Acinonyx jubatus*. The IUCN Red List of Threatened Species. Version 2022-2. https://www.iucnredlist.org. Downloaded on 13.2.2023.
African golden cat. IUCN (International Union for Conservation of Nature) 2015. *Caracal aurata*. The IUCN Red List of Threatened Species. Version 2022-2. https://www.iucnredlist.org. Downloaded on 13.2.2023.

Caracal. IUCN (International Union for Conservation of Nature) 2016. *Caracal caracal.* The IUCN Red List of Threatened Species. Version 2022-2. https://www.iucnredlist.org. Downloaded on 13.2.2023.
Leopard. Peter Gerngross 2019. *Panthera pardus.* The IUCN Red List of Threatened Species. Version 2022-2. https://www.iucnredlist.org. Downloaded on 13.2.2023.
Serval. IUCN (International Union for Conservation of Nature) 2015. *Leptailurus serval.* The IUCN Red List of Threatened Species. Version 2022-2. https://www.iucnredlist.org. Downloaded on 13.2.2023.
Common genet. IUCN (International Union for Conservation of Nature) 2008. *Genetta genetta.* The IUCN Red List of Threatened Species. Version 2022-2. https://www.iucnredlist.org. Downloaded on 13.2.2023.
African civet. IUCN (International Union for Conservation of Nature) 2011. *Civettictis civetta.* The IUCN Red List of Threatened Species. Version 2022-2. https://www.iucnredlist.org. Downloaded on 13.2.2023.
Afro-asiatic wildcat. Ghoddousi et al. 2022. *Felis lybica.* The IUCN Red List of Threatened Species. Version 2022-2. https://www.iucnredlist.org. Downloaded on 13.2.2023.
Aardwolf. IUCN (International Union for Conservation of Nature) 2015. *Proteles cristata.* The IUCN Red List of Threatened Species. Version 2022-2. https://www.iucnredlist.org. Downloaded on 22.2.2023.
Spotted hyena. IUCN (International Union for Conservation of Nature) 2015. *Crocuta crocuta.* The IUCN Red List of Threatened Species. Version 2022-2. https://www.iucnredlist.org. Downloaded on 22.2.2023.
Striped hyena. IUCN (International Union for Conservation of Nature) 2015. *Hyaena hyaena.* The IUCN Red List of Threatened Species. Version 2022-2. https://www.iucnredlist.org. Downloaded on 22.2.2023.
Honey badger. IUCN (International Union for Conservation of Nature) 2016. *Mellivora capensis.* The IUCN Red List of Threatened Species. Version 2022-2. https://www.iucnredlist.org. Downloaded on 22.2.2023.
African wolf. UCN (International Union for Conservation of Nature) 2018. *Canis lupaster.* The IUCN Red List of Threatened Species. Version 2022-2. https://www.iucnredlist.org. Downloaded on 22.2.2023.
Bat-eared fox. IUCN (International Union for Conservation of Nature) 2014. *Otocyon megalotis.* The IUCN Red List of Threatened Species. Version 2022-2. https://www.iucnredlist.org. Downloaded on 24.2.2023.
Side-striped jackal. IUCN (International Union for Conservation of Nature) 2008. *Canis adustus.* The IUCN Red List of Threatened Species. Version 2022-2. https://www.iucnredlist.org. Downloaded on 24.2.2023.
Black-backed jackal. IUCN (International Union for Conservation of Nature) 2008. *Canis mesomelas.* The IUCN Red List of Threatened Species. Version 2022-2. https://www.iucnredlist.org. Downloaded on 24.2.2023.
African wild dog. IUCN (International Union for Conservation of Nature) 2008. *Lycaon pictus.* The IUCN Red List of Threatened Species. Version 2022-2. https://www.iucnredlist.org. Downloaded on 24.2.2023.
Lesser kudu. IUCN (International Union for Conservation of Nature) 2008. *Tragelaphus imberbis.* The IUCN Red List of Threatened Species. Version 2022-2. https://www.iucnredlist.org. Downloaded on 27.2.2023.
Fringe-eared oryx. IUCN (International Union for Conservation of Nature) 2018. *Oryx beisa ssp. callotis.* The IUCN Red List of Threatened Species. Version 2022-2. https://www.iucnredlist.org. Downloaded on 27.2.2023.
Gerenuk. IUCN (International Union for Conservation of Nature) 2008. *Litocranius walleri.* The IUCN Red List of Threatened Species. Version 2022-2. https://www.iucnredlist.org. Downloaded on 27.2.2023.
Thomson's gazelle. IUCN (International Union for Conservation of Nature) 2008. *Eudorcas thomsonii.* The IUCN Red List of Threatened Species. Version 2022-2. https://www.iucnredlist.org. Downloaded on 27.2.2023.
Grant's gezelle. IUCN (International Union for Conservation of Nature) 2008. *Nanger granti.* The IUCN Red List of Threatened Species. Version 2022-2. https://www.iucnredlist.org. Downloaded on 27.2.2023.
Hippopotamus. IUCN (International Union for Conservation of Nature) 2017. *Hippopotamus amphibius.* The IUCN Red List of Threatened Species. Version 2022-2. https://www.iucnredlist.org. Downloaded on 28.2.2023.
Nile crodocile. Isberg, S.R., Combrink, X., Lippai, C., Balaguera-Reina, S. & Ross, J.P. 2018. *Crocodylus niloticus.* The IUCN Red List of Threatened Species. Version 2022-2. https://www.iucnredlist.org. Downloaded on 28.2.2023.
African clawless otter. IUCN (International Union for Conservation of Nature) 2015. *Aonyx capensis.* The IUCN Red List of Threatened Species. Version 2022-2. https://www.iucnredlist.org. Downloaded on 28.2.2023.
Spotted-necked otter. IUCN (International Union for Conservation of Nature) 2015. *Hydrictis maculicollis.* The IUCN Red List of Threatened Species. Version 2022-2. https://www.iucnredlist.org. Downloaded on 28.2.2023.
Vervet monkey. IUCN (International Union for Conservation of Nature) 2022. *Chlorocebus pygerythrus.* The IUCN Red List of Threatened Species. Version 2022-2. https://www.iucnredlist.org. Downloaded on 28.2.2023.

Eastern gorilla. IGCP and WCS 2019. *Gorilla beringei. The IUCN Red List of Threatened Species.* Version 2022-2. https://www.iucnredlist.org. Downloaded on 28.2.2023.
Chimpanzee. IUCN SSC A.P.E.S. Database; Jane Goodall Institute, UNEP-WCMC 2018. *Pan troglodytes. The IUCN Red List of Threatened Species.* Version 2022-2. https://www.iucnredlist.org. Downloaded on 28.2.2023.
Olive baboon. Janette Wallis and IUCN (International Union for Conservation of Nature) 2020. *Papio anubis. The IUCN Red List of Threatened Species.* Version 2022-2. https://www.iucnredlist.org. Downloaded on 28.2.2023.
Yellow baboon. Janette Wallis and IUCN (International Union for Conservation of Nature) 2020. *Papio cynocephalus. The IUCN Red List of Threatened Species.* Version 2022-2. https://www.iucnredlist.org. Downloaded on 28.2.2023.
Angolan colobus. Yvonne de Jong, Tom Butynski and IUCN (International Union for Conservation of Nature) 2020. *Colobus angolensis. The IUCN Red List of Threatened Species.* Version 2022-2. https://www.iucnredlist.org. Downloaded on 28.2.2023.
Guereza. IUCN (International Union for Conservation of Nature) 2019. *Colobus guereza. The IUCN Red List of Threatened Species.* Version 2022-2. https://www.iucnredlist.org. Downloaded on 28.2.2023.
Mt. Kilimanjaro guereza. IUCN (International Union for Conservation of Nature) 2020. *Colobus caudatus. The IUCN Red List of Threatened Species.* Version 2022-2. https://www.iucnredlist.org. Downloaded on 28.2.2023.
Tana river red colobus. WCS - Tanzania; IUCN (International Union for Conservation of Nature) 2018. *Piliocolobus rufomitratus. The IUCN Red List of Threatened Species.* Version 2022-2. https://www.iucnredlist.org. Downloaded on 28.2.2023.
Zanzibar red colobus. IUCN (International Union for Conservation of Nature) 2017. *Piliocolobus kirkii. The IUCN Red List of Threatened Species.* Version 2022-2. https://www.iucnredlist.org. Downloaded on 28.2.2023.
Udzungwa red colobus. IUCN (International Union for Conservation of Nature) 2019. *Piliocolobus gordonorum. The IUCN Red List of Threatened Species.* Version 2022-2. https://www.iucnredlist.org. Downloaded on 28.2.2023.
Ashy red colobus. Red Colobus (Piliocolobus) Conservation Action Plan, 2020–2025. 2020. *Piliocolobus tephrosceles. The IUCN Red List of Threatened Species.* Version 2022-2. https://www.iucnredlist.org. Downloaded on 28.2.2023.
Blue monkey. Yvonne de Jong, Tom Butynski and IUCN (International Union for Conservation of Nature) 2021. *Cercopithecus mitis. The IUCN Red List of Threatened Species.* Version 2022-2. https://www.iucnredlist.org. Downloaded on 28.2.2023.
Red-tailed monkey. IUCN (International Union for Conservation of Nature) 2019. *Cercopithecus ascanius. The IUCN Red List of Threatened Species.* Version 2022-2. https://www.iucnredlist.org. Downloaded on 28.2.2023.
Zorilla. IUCN (International Union for Conservation of Nature) 2008. *Ictonyx striatus. The IUCN Red List of Threatened Species.* Version 2022-2. https://www.iucnredlist.org. Downloaded on 3.3.2023.
Aardvark. IUCN (International Union for Conservation of Nature) 2015. *Orycteropus afer. The IUCN Red List of Threatened Species.* Version 2022-2. https://www.iucnredlist.org. Downloaded on 3.3.2023.
Temminck's pangolin. IUCN SSC Pangolin Specialist Group 2019. *Smutsia temminckii. The IUCN Red List of Threatened Species.* Version 2022-2. https://www.iucnredlist.org. Downloaded on 3.3.2023.
Giant gound pangolin. IUCN SSC Pangolin Specialist Group 2019. *Smutsia gigantea. The IUCN Red List of Threatened Species.* Version 2022-2. https://www.iucnredlist.org. Downloaded on 3.3.2023.
White-bellied pangolin. IUCN SSC Pangolin Specialist Group 2019. *Phataginus tricuspis. The IUCN Red List of Threatened Species.* Version 2022-2. https://www.iucnredlist.org. Downloaded on 3.3.2023.
Demidoff's dwarf galago. IUCN (International Union for Conservation of Nature) 2019. *Galagoides demidoff. The IUCN Red List of Threatened Species.* Version 2022-2. https://www.iucnredlist.org. Downloaded on 3.3.2023.
Thick-tailed greater galago. IUCN (International Union for Conservation of Nature) 2019. *Otolemur crassicaudatus. The IUCN Red List of Threatened Species.* Version 2022-2. https://www.iucnredlist.org. Downloaded on 3.3.2023.
Garnett's greater galago. IUCN (International Union for Conservation of Nature) 2019. *Otolemur garnettii. The IUCN Red List of Threatened Species.* Version 2022-2. https://www.iucnredlist.org. Downloaded on 3.3.2023.
Northern lesser galago. IUCN (International Union for Conservation of Nature) 2019. *Galago senegalensis. The IUCN Red List of Threatened Species.* Version 2022-2. https://www.iucnredlist.org. Downloaded on 3.3.2023.
Somali lesser galago. IUCN (International Union for Conservation of Nature) 2019. *Galago gallarum. The IUCN Red List of Threatened Species.* Version 2022-2. https://www.iucnredlist.org. Downloaded on 3.3.2023.
Four-toed hedgehog. IUCN (International Union for Conservation of Nature) 2008. *Atelerix albiventris. The IUCN Red List of Threatened Species.* Version 2022-2. https://www.iucnredlist.org. Downloaded on 3.3.2023.
Crested porcupine. IUCN (International Union for Conservation of Nature) 2014. *Hystrix cristata. The IUCN Red List of Threatened Species.* Version 2022-2. https://www.iucnredlist.org. Downloaded on 3.3.2023.

Cape porcupine. IUCN (International Union for Conservation of Nature) 2008. *Hystrix africaeaustralis*. The IUCN Red List of Threatened Species. Version 2022-2. https://www.iucnredlist.org. Downloaded on 3.3.2023.

African brush-tailed porcupine. IUCN (International Union for Conservation of Nature) 2008. *Atherurus africanus*. The IUCN Red List of Threatened Species. Version 2022-2. https://www.iucnredlist.org. Downloaded on 3.3.2023.

African striped weasel. IUCN (International Union for Conservation of Nature) 2008. *Poecilogale albinucha*. The IUCN Red List of Threatened Species. Version 2022-2. https://www.iucnredlist.org. Downloaded on 3.3.2023.

Bushpig. IUCN (International Union for Conservation of Nature) 2016. *Potamochoerus larvatus*. The IUCN Red List of Threatened Species. Version 2022-2. https://www.iucnredlist.org. Downloaded on 6.3.2023.

Red river hog. IUCN (International Union for Conservation of Nature) 2016. *Potamochoerus porcus*. The IUCN Red List of Threatened Species. Version 2022-2. https://www.iucnredlist.org. Downloaded on 6.3.2023.

Common warthog. IUCN (International Union for Conservation of Nature) 2016. *Phacochoerus africanus*. The IUCN Red List of Threatened Species. Version 2022-2. https://www.iucnredlist.org. Downloaded on 6.3.2023.

Desert warthog. de Jong, Y.A., d'Huart, J., Butynski, T.M., Culverwell, J., Feely, J., Bell-Cross, S., Caron, A., King, J., Pohlstrand, H., Dufresne, H., Williams, S., Mallon, D., Hamerlynck, O., Luke, Q., Trailin, V. and Grubb, P. 2001. 2016. *Phacochoerus aethiopicus*. The IUCN Red List of Threatened Species. Version 2022-2. https://www.iucnredlist.org. Downloaded on 6.3.2023.

Forest hog. IUCN (International Union for Conservation of Nature) 2016. *Hylochoerus meinertzhageni*. The IUCN Red List of Threatened Species. Version 2022-2. https://www.iucnredlist.org. Downloaded on 6.3.2023.

Rock hyrax. IUCN (International Union for Conservation of Nature) 2015. *Procavia capensis*. The IUCN Red List of Threatened Species. Version 2022-2. https://www.iucnredlist.org. Downloaded on 13.3.2023.

Easter tree hyrax. IUCN (International Union for Conservation of Nature) 2015. *Dendrohyrax validus*. The IUCN Red List of Threatened Species. Version 2022-2. https://www.iucnredlist.org. Downloaded on 13.3.2023.

Bush hyrax. IUCN (International Union for Conservation of Nature) 2015. *Heterohyrax brucei*. The IUCN Red List of Threatened Species. Version 2022-2. https://www.iucnredlist.org. Downloaded on 13.3.2023.

Western tree hyrax. IUCN (International Union for Conservation of Nature) 2015. *Dendrohyrax dorsalis*. The IUCN Red List of Threatened Species. Version 2022-2. https://www.iucnredlist.org. Downloaded on 13.3.2023.

Southern tree hyrax. IUCN (International Union for Conservation of Nature) 2015. *Dendrohyrax arboreus*. The IUCN Red List of Threatened Species. Version 2022-2. https://www.iucnredlist.org. Downloaded on 13.3.2023.

Banded mongoose. IUCN (International Union for Conservation of Nature) 2016. *Mungos mungo*. The IUCN Red List of Threatened Species. Version 2022-2. https://www.iucnredlist.org. Downloaded on 13.3.2023.

African savanna hare. IUCN (International Union for Conservation of Nature) 2019. *Lepus victoriae*. The IUCN Red List of Threatened Species. Version 2022-2. https://www.iucnredlist.org. Downloaded on 13.3.2023.

Abyssinian hare. IUCN (International Union for Conservation of Nature) 2019. *Lepus habessinicus*. The IUCN Red List of Threatened Species. Version 2022-2. https://www.iucnredlist.org. Downloaded on 13.3.2023.

Cape hare. IUCN (International Union for Conservation of Nature) 2019. *Lepus capensis*. The IUCN Red List of Threatened Species. Version 2022-2. https://www.iucnredlist.org. Downloaded on 13.3.2023.

Large-spotted genet. IUCN (International Union for Conservation of Nature) 2016. *Genetta maculata*. The IUCN Red List of Threatened Species. Version 2022-2. https://www.iucnredlist.org. Downloaded on 13.3.2023.

Pygmy scaly-tailed flying squirrel. IUCN (International Union for Conservation of Nature) 2008. *Idiurus zenkeri*. The IUCN Red List of Threatened Species. Version 2022-2. https://www.iucnredlist.org. Downloaded on 14.4.2023.

Striped ground squirrel. IUCN (International Union for Conservation of Nature) 2008. *Xerus erythropus*. The IUCN Red List of Threatened Species. Version 2022-2. https://www.iucnredlist.org. Downloaded on 14.4.2023.

Gambian sun squirrel. IUCN (International Union for Conservation of Nature) 2008. *Heliosciurus gambianus*. The IUCN Red List of Threatened Species. Version 2022-2. https://www.iucnredlist.org. Downloaded on 14.4.2023.

Boehm's bush squirrel. IUCN (International Union for Conservation of Nature) 2008. *Paraxerus boehmi*. The IUCN Red List of Threatened Species. Version 2022-2. https://www.iucnredlist.org. Downloaded on 14.4.2023.

Unstriped ground squirrel. IUCN (International Union for Conservation of Nature) 2008. *Xerus rutilus*. The IUCN Red List of Threatened Species. Version 2022-2. https://www.iucnredlist.org. Downloaded on 14.4.2023.

Lord Derby's scaly-tailed squirrel. IUCN (International Union for Conservation of Nature) 2008. *Anomalurus derbianus*. The IUCN Red List of Threatened Species. Version 2022-2. https://www.iucnredlist.org. Downloaded on 14.4.2023.

Red bush squirrel. IUCN (International Union for Conservation of Nature) 2008. *Paraxerus palliatus. The IUCN Red List of Threatened Species.* Version 2022-2. https://www.iucnredlist.org. Downloaded on 14.4.2023.
Carruther's mountain squirrel. IUCN (International Union for Conservation of Nature) 2008. *Funisciurus carruthersi. The IUCN Red List of Threatened Species.* Version 2022-2. https://www.iucnredlist.org. Downloaded on 14.4.2023.
Forest giant squirrel. IUCN (International Union for Conservation of Nature) 2008. *Protoxerus stangeri. The IUCN Red List of Threatened Species.* Version 2022-2. https://www.iucnredlist.org. Downloaded on 14.4.2023.
Swynnerton's bush squirrel. IUCN SSC Small Mammal Specialist Group 2019. *Paraxerus vexillarius. The IUCN Red List of Threatened Species.* Version 2022-2. https://www.iucnredlist.org. Downloaded on 14.4.2023.
Zanj sun squirrel. IUCN (International Union for Conservation of Nature) 2008. *Heliosciurus undulatus. The IUCN Red List of Threatened Species.* Version 2022-2. https://www.iucnredlist.org. Downloaded on 14.4.2023.
Mutable sun squirrel. IUCN (International Union for Conservation of Nature) 2008. *Heliosciurus mutabilis. The IUCN Red List of Threatened Species.* Version 2022-2. https://www.iucnredlist.org. Downloaded on 14.4.2023.
Ochre bush squirrel. IUCN (International Union for Conservation of Nature) 2008. *Paraxerus ochraceus. The IUCN Red List of Threatened Species.* Version 2022-2. https://www.iucnredlist.org. Downloaded on 14.4.2023.
Alexander's bush squirrel. IUCN (International Union for Conservation of Nature) 2008. *Paraxerus alexandri. The IUCN Red List of Threatened Species.* Version 2022-2. https://www.iucnredlist.org. Downloaded on 14.4.2023.
Pygmy scaly-tailed flying squirrel. IUCN (International Union for Conservation of Nature) 2008. *Idiurus zenkeri. The IUCN Red List of Threatened Species.* Version 2022-2. https://www.iucnredlist.org. Downloaded on 14.4.2023.
Striped bush squirrel. IUCN (International Union for Conservation of Nature) 2008. *Paraxerus flavovittis. The IUCN Red List of Threatened Species.* Version 2022-2. https://www.iucnredlist.org. Downloaded on 14.4.2023.
Ruwenzori sun sqirrel. IUCN (International Union for Conservation of Nature) 2008. *Heliosciurus ruwenzorii. The IUCN Red List of Threatened Species.* Version 2022-2. https://www.iucnredlist.org. Downloaded on 14.4.2023.
Smith's bush squirrel. IUCN (International Union for Conservation of Nature) 2008. *Paraxerus cepapi. The IUCN Red List of Threatened Species.* Version 2022-2. https://www.iucnredlist.org. Downloaded on 14.4.2023.
Somali ostrich. BirdLife International and Handbook of the Birds of the World (2020). 2022. *Struthio molybdophanes. The IUCN Red List of Threatened Species.* Version 2022-2. https://www.iucnredlist.org. Downloaded on 21.4.2023.
Common ostrich. BirdLife International and Handbook of the Birds of the World (2018). 2017. *Struthio camelus. The IUCN Red List of Threatened Species.* Version 2022-2. https://www.iucnredlist.org. Downloaded on 21.4.2023.

Bibliography
Estes, R. D. The Behaviour Guide to African Mammals. South Africa 1995
Estes, R. D. The Safari Companion - a Guide to watching African Mammals. South Africa 1999
Hedges, N. G. Reptiles and Amphibians of East Africa. Kenya 1983
Richmond, M.D. (ed.) The Seashores of Eastern Africa and the Western Indian Ocean Islands. Tanzania 2022
Spawls, S., Howell, K., Drewes, R., Ashe, J. A Field Guide to the Reptiles of East Africa. Academic Press 2002
Stevenson, T., Fanshawe, J. Field Guide to the Birds of East Africa. London 2002
Stuart, C. & T. A Field Guide to the Tracks & Signs of Southern and East African Wildlife. South Africa 1994

The author

Raised in Germany, Birgit was caught by the travel bug early on and has lived half of her life as an expat - in South Africa, Tanzania, Switzerland, and now in Scotland.

After graduating in Germany with a master's degree in geography (Diplomgeographin), she moved to Tanzania in 1999, where she spent years in the bush mapping wildlife areas. While raising her children, she worked as a GIS analyst in nature conservation and as a free-lance designer. Painting and drawing in her spare time, her works have been exhibited in Germany, Morocco, Tanzania and South Africa.

Combining her experience in different countries, her geographic studies and her passion for photography, writing, art and design, she currently works as a freelance writer and designer on a variety of projects for clients all over the globe.

www.ingramcontent.com/pod-product-compliance
Lightning Source LLC
Chambersburg PA
CBHW060459010526
44118CB00018B/2467